Praise for *Break into Modeling for Under $20*

"I have been working in the modeling business most of my life. I judged the Miss Universe, Miss America, and Miss USA pageants, along with all the years of working with actors, actresses, models, singers, and talent contests. Judy Goss tells it the way it needs to be told. Whatever a person has to do to buy this book, it's worth the price. This is the quintessential book for a struggling newcomer on how to really do it."   —Robert Metzgar, producer at MCA Universal

"Judy Goss is a true professional when it comes to understanding the modeling business. *Break into Modeling for Under $20* is brilliant and a must-read no matter what type of model you are and no matter your age or experience. Judy gives expert insider advice that you need to know before spending a dollar if you are really serious about becoming a model."   —Tamsen Fadal, TV personality and author of
Why Hasn't He Called?

"Judy Goss has deployed her hands-on experience and considerable expertise to provide a unique look into the business aspects of the modeling industry. Judy shatters common misperceptions and demystifies the world of high fashion. She lays out an understandable and attainable path to a career as a model. This is a must-read."
—Arnold P. Peter, entertainment lawyer at
Raskin Peter Rubin & Simon, LLP

"*Break into Modeling for Under $20* is the greatest gift given in the modeling industry. Follow Judy's advice, and your dream may become a reality like mine did!"
—Lani Ridenhour, model at the Bella Agency, New York

"This is *the* book for all models from an insider that knows how the industry works inside and out."
—Marta Tracy, TV and digital media PR strategist,
executive producer, and coauthor of *Starring You!*

BREAK INTO MODELING

FOR UNDER $20

BREAK INTO MODELING

FOR UNDER
$20

JUDY GOSS

 St. Martin's Griffin ⬭ New York

BREAK INTO MODELING FOR UNDER $20. Copyright © 2008 by Judy Goss. All rights reserved. Printed in the United States of America. For information, address St. Martin's Press, 175 Fifth Avenue, New York, N.Y. 10010.

www.stmartins.com

Design by Susan Walsh

Library of Congress Cataloging-in-Publication Data

Goss, Judy.
  Break into modeling for under $20 / Judy Goss.—1st ed.
    p. cm.
  ISBN-13: 978-0-312-37260-6
  ISBN-10: 0-312-37260-4
  1. Models (Persons)—Vocational guidance.   I. Title.

HD6073.M77 G67 2008
746.9'2023—dc22   2008013008

First Edition: August 2008

10 9 8 7 6 5 4 3 2 1

To my husband, Bruce, our twins,
Danielle and Dara, and my stepson, Dylan

—the four of you are not only beautiful on the outside, but fit the
description of a model family from within, as well.

CONTENTS

▪ ▪ ▪ ▪

ACKNOWLEDGMENTS

■ ■ ■ ■

Thank you to all of the superagents and industry professionals who helped me with this book, especially Nathalie Bernier, Soni Ekvall, Jill Joyce, Angelo Laudisa, Marsha McMorrough, Rosie Niku, Stacy Rosen, Julia Samersova, and Ray Volant. Your passion for the business and willingness to help me with information, models, or quotes was endless! Also, thank you to my gorgeous model friends Chantal Bolivar and Helen Powers—you helped me see things from different perspectives and your input was truly an inspiration to me.

Another heartfelt thank-you to Jennifer Weis and Hilary Rubin from St. Martin's Press, whose encouragement and leadership influenced me to create chapters in this book that went far beyond my original intention, and also a big thank-you to Stefanie Lindskog from St. Martin's Press, for painstakingly guiding me through the writing process and keeping me on the right track.

To Cindi Blair and Robert Metzgar, without you two caring so much about this project, it would never have been born. Thank you for the pivotal advice you gave to me in the beginning.

A special thank-you goes out to Steve Cohen from St. Martin's Press, who was the first to see my vision of this book in its entirety.

And finally, I can't express enough the gratitude I feel for my husband and his infinite patience in taking care of our twin toddlers when my face was buried in the computer for weeks at a time. I truly am the lucky one!

BREAK INTO
MODELING

FOR UNDER
$20

INTRODUCTION

■ ■ ■ ■

Welcome to the World of Modeling!

You are about to be walked through the simplest and least expensive way to enter into the modeling world, the way to break into the business *preferred* by modeling agencies. This book will show you how to be your own manager. These techniques are the ones used by modeling scouts and managers who place new models with agencies all over the world every day.

The information I give you *has never before* been published in such simple detail for the general public. Why not? One reason is because modeling conventions and schools would lose money if everyone tried to break in the *real* way—then they wouldn't be able to charge you for making contacts that you could otherwise make yourself. And I'll show you how to make many more connections in addition to what they could provide. Plus, conventions and schools make money off workshops that offer the same information I provide right here in this book (such as how to dress and what questions to ask when you go on an agency open call, and about the modeling industry in general). This book will teach you more than a weekend modeling convention with workshops *and* a semester of school about modeling combined, and for a fraction of the cost—not to mention advice on how to make valuable contacts on your own. People who work at modeling agencies are incredibly busy, and they simply don't have the time to explain this process to everyone who walks through their doors or sends them pictures. Now, all you need to know to break into the modeling industry has finally been condensed into four easy steps—preparation, pictures, promotion, presentation—that you can follow at your leisure, along with all of the extra know-how about the industry that is crucial to your being a part of it.

I come from twenty years of experience in the fashion industry: I worked as a high-fashion model for several years with Ford Models in New York City and have also had several years of experience as an agent at two of the top-ten high-fashion agencies in the world, including New York Models and Ford NY (yes, I became an agent on their celebrity board long after I was a model with them). In addition I have been a casting director, bookings editor for two national magazines, art buyer, producer, manager, and scout—all in New York City. I also worked at a modeling convention company at one point, so I can let you in on the secrets from *every* angle possible.

In addition to my easy four-step process, I will also give you tips on how to pose for the camera, common insider scams to stay away from that do not get publicized enough, valuable leads to reputable modeling agencies around the world with specific e-mails and marketing advice, and interviews with and quotes from some high-profile casting directors, models, and expert modeling agents to help you on your way to becoming a model. Some of the advice may even prove useful *after* you snag an agency for representation: how to present yourself at an open call or casting, how to request financial assistance from an agency ahead of time (especially if you are traveling to a different city to live), and so on.

At the end of the book, I've also included important business tips you can apply to your new career, an explanation of insider industry terms to help you speak the lingo, important advice for parents who may be considering a modeling career for their children, as well as follow-up advice—*whether or not* you find an agency to represent you.

If these techniques do not work the first time, do *not* give up, but just repeat the whole process in eight weeks. The modeling business has certain "looks" that come and go, and you could be the next type they are looking for at any given time! If you don't get in the first time, you have a better chance at getting in with another attempt by building on your experience and creating your look to work for you by following these simple steps.

When I started my career in modeling, I approached Ford Models *five* times at their open calls in New York before they finally accepted me. Plus, as a manager I have personally placed girls without *any* professional pictures or experience in the industry with agencies around the world, sending only the types of pictures I will show you how to take. In one case, an agency advanced—to more than one girl—overseas plane fare, hotel accommodations, photo shoots to start a portfolio, *plus* composites! And it's not that agencies gave me the time of day because they knew who I was; I just was aware of what specific pictures I should send to get their attention. I have also placed a fifty-year-old woman with white hair at one of the best and biggest commercial print agencies in New York City. She then moved from North Carolina to start her career as a model, and became very successful, so the spectrum of the business is probably broader than you think.

My four-step process of breaking into the modeling industry is described as follows:

1. **PREPARATION:** how to prepare yourself mentally and physically for breaking into the world of modeling, how to realistically figure out what type of model you are. I also provide an overview about how modeling agencies work.
2. **PICTURES:** how to take the proper photos—including poses, dress, angles, and lighting—that all modeling agencies are looking for.
3. **PROMOTION:** tips on how to sell yourself to modeling agencies *all over the world,* and how to find those agencies, for your specific look.
4. **PRESENTATION:** the optimum way to present yourself at a modeling agency—what to wear, what to say, what questions to ask whether or not they want you to, and how to act, as well as a glimpse into exactly what happens on an open call or a request meeting with a modeling agency.

Please follow these steps precisely, one by one, for maximum efficiency. There are no guarantees, as with any business, but following these steps exactly will give you an edge in breaking into such a highly competitive industry. And make sure to read the entire book before starting the Four-P process, then go back through and focus on the four steps meticulously.

Your First Reality Check

Almost everyone has heard or read stories about the modeling industry. The press covers both extremes—not only the glamorous side of modeling, such as travel to exotic lands, getting paid thousands of dollars for one day's work, and the benefits of fame and fortune, but also the pitfalls of modeling, the stories of tragic drug addiction and extreme eating disorders. These sensational stories may attract readers and sell tabloids to the public, but they do not give you any idea about how to actually get yourself *into* the modeling industry, or better yet, what is the best way to attract the attention of people within the industry. The gossip and stories are fun, but modeling is still a business, and should be treated as such.

Before we start my 4-P process, there are several things I can teach you that will not only help you get ready for this business as a newcomer, but that can also be used *after* an agency or manager selects you and you are well on your way to a successful modeling career. The way to pose for a picture and prepare for castings (which are some of the things I cover in detail) does not change after you actually start working in the business. If you are already working in the industry but are with a modeling agency in a small town or city and want to expand your search for a modeling agency beyond your agency's capabilities, if you need to change agencies and don't have a manager to market you, or if you simply want to know the marketing concepts and lingo of modeling so you can keep tabs on how your agency is marketing you, this process will help you. You will always be coming back to the basics I'm going to teach you because they will become the base of everything you eventually are involved in as a model.

Let me first tell you about the number one rule in the modeling industry, a rule that I will keep repeating throughout this book: *no one* should have to pay money *up front* to be in the modeling industry. Sure, it will cost you money for the pictures in your portfolio, the pictured composites you give to clients, and other business expenses (which I show you how to get help with from the agencies later on in this book), but these expenses are all incurred *after* you are in the business and have representation at a legitimate modeling agency or with a model manager. (I explain the difference between agencies and managers in chapter 7 under "Agency Versus Manager" in "Terms You Should Know.")

If you doubt this, just pick up the phone and call *any legitimate modeling agency worldwide* and ask them if you need to send professional pictures to their agency as a potential new model. The answer will *always* be no. If you are still skeptical, then keep reading, because I am excited to show you the *real* way to break into modeling for hardly any money at all!

Are you thinking that you have already gone down that road and paid money for someone to "market you" who did not work at a modeling agency? These fees are bogusly called "registration" or "consultation" fees. Or perhaps you paid for "photo packages" from someone, or had a credit card submitted for an automatic monthly fee for a Web site that did not get you any castings or contacts. If so, just move forward from here with my advice. To try and save your money you should immediately cancel your "subscription" on any Web site that isn't directly affiliated with a reputable modeling agency, or get a refund from a photo package that you purchased if you haven't gone on the actual shoot yet. These are *not* legitimate ways to break into the modeling industry. Actually, paying someone ahead of time is never a legitimate way to get into a modeling agency. This is very well known *within* the modeling industry, but most outsiders do not understand that you can get proper exposure to agencies worldwide for virtually no money.

Plus, the way I will teach you how to dress, have pictures taken of yourself, and then how to send those pictures out to modeling agencies is *preferred* by the agencies rather than you spending your money. It's as easy as taking a picture with the family camera in your backyard, printing it on your own printer, and then sending it in the mail! I go into further detail about unnecessary expenses (which more often than not are scams) in chapter 6, but for now, just realize that you should not pay *any* money up front to anyone *before* you acquire representation from a modeling agency.

If you do not get into a modeling agency directly, a manager or scout could propose you. A manager is someone who not only oversees a modeling career but also places models with agencies, as opposed to a scout, who solely places models with agencies. The manager or scout *still* shouldn't charge you, because the modeling agency you sign with will give them a fee for their services (for the scouts) or a percentage of your earnings (to the managers). Model managers may not charge *you,* but agencies have to split your future commissions with them. So modeling agencies prefer to take on new faces without any previous ties, so they can manage the person's career directly themselves and not have to share any commissions. So if you can get started without a manager, why shouldn't you?

There certainly isn't anything *wrong* with getting a model manager to help you get into a modeling agency. Along with agents and scouts, model managers are also suitable channels for getting yourself into the modeling industry. But though managers are great to help develop and guide a career in modeling, at least try the process I teach you first, to see how far you can go without a manager. Then if you don't get the response you want and you catch a manager's attention along the way, he or she can take you a step further and help develop you appropriately for representation. But don't be surprised when a manager uses the same tools for marketing you that I mention in this book!

Your Advantage to Breaking into This Industry in the Twenty-first Century

The era of the "supermodel" has been gone since before the turn of the century, and this helps you immensely. Why? Because the whole spectrum of the modeling industry has changed, allowing more room for all different types of models to make more money. Back then, only a handful of girls were "supermodels," and other than the supermodels, only a small group of girls made notable salaries. A typical "model" had to fall within a few very specific requirements (similar to those who were supermodels) to be considered a model. All of the "big" money used to go to the chosen supermodels of that particular decade, and no one else. And very few chosen models (besides the supermodels) used to grace cover after cover after cover in the high-end fashion magazines, which left barely any work for the rest of the models. Plus, there weren't nearly as many magazines being published (or advertisements being shown) as there are now, so the odds of getting attention as a model were much smaller.

To be a "supermodel" today, you don't need to be a household name, such as Heidi Klum, Naomi Campbell, or Christie Brinkley. Nowadays, there are so many various kinds of models in all different categories (including age, size, height, and ethnicity) who have the ability to make upward of six figures, as well as being touted as a "supermodel" by the press. There are even some models making solid six-figure salaries, and the public may never even know their names. They may never even appear in front of the camera! Yes, you can technically be a "model," and not ever have your picture taken for public use. Fit and showroom models (explained in the "Categories of Modeling" section in chapter 1) rarely have their pictures taken for the public eye, though they are both bona fide categories of the modeling industry. One fit model that I interview later in this book, Helen Powers, has been making upward of *$300,000 per year* for many years, and the public doesn't know who she is, because she works behind the scenes at various designers' and manufacturers' offices. Don't worry, these different types of modeling will all make sense after you read this book, and I will show you how to access these jobs if you are the appropriate type.

The types of work available for models have recently increased dramatically. There are of course the typical megafamous models, such as Gisele Bündchen, Kate Moss, and Heidi Klum, who have arisen over the past decade to grace the covers of magazines and grab the higher profile campaigns for millions of dollars, but these types of models are becoming more and more scarce. Even though Gisele, Kate, and Heidi are examples of your modern-day supermodels, there is still *plenty* of work left for the rest of you, which wasn't the case until the past few years or so. The definition of "supermodel" has been broken wide open, for there are now male, plus-size, and runway "supermodels" who specialize in their own categories. Many more people now have a chance at being a part of the bigger picture in the modeling industry.

Julia Samersova, a casting director in New York City for high-fashion print clients (as well as a former scout at Ford Models and modeling agent at Next Models and Elite Models in New York), says that these days the industry is about "spirit, personality, and energy more than a certain type of look. Don't get me wrong, you still have to be thin to be in high fashion, because at the end of the day the designers want a beautiful hanger, but there just isn't one specific look anymore—I really do believe that." The bulk of the models today can more easily make six figures and up—even if you are not in the high-fashion arena. Reality shows have also helped make celebrities out of "average" types of people, and in that respect have opened doors for many other types of people to be a part of the ever changing modeling industry, which makes all different types of people more acceptable for advertising in the public eye. In addition, actors, musicians, and other celebrities, like sports personalities, are in advertising campaigns and commercials. This diversity trickles down into the modeling world, resulting in a broader acceptance of the idea that more varied types of people can publicize products. Also, the number of products being advertised is greatly increasing, with actors creating fragrance products, musicians developing clothing lines, and let's face it—the more marketing that is done all over the world, the more work there is for noncelebrities like you and me!

The Many Types of Models

I like to call the modeling industry just that instead of the "fashion industry" because models help sell everything these days, from couture gowns to automobiles. This industry has exploded, with people of all different sizes and characteristics working as models. For example, in the past the average-size female never had much of a chance at modeling, because the requirements of modeling only included smaller dress sizes on very tall bodies, but work has substantially increased in the plus-size modeling arena (which *starts* at size ten and goes up to size twenty-four), as well as fit modeling, which frequently demands a height of five seven or five eight. These two areas alone reel in people who have closer to average sizes and measurements and are not typical high-fashion material.

The commercial print sector has a demand for more and more people that are a *minimum* of thirty-five years of age. It entails mainly advertising "products" other than clothing. If you set aside clothing advertising, commercial print is advertising for just about every other inanimate object that you can see! This is a *huge* market for the average person who does not fit under the high-fashion umbrella (either because of measurement restrictions or age). If you look around, it is very common to see "real people" everywhere in advertising. And my guess is that commercial print modeling is going to get even more popular, and the demand for older models will be ever increasing because of the wave of advertising that is going to be focused toward the baby boomer population in the coming years.

Both the men's arena of modeling along with plus-size modeling have also increased monumentally in recent years, resulting in an increase in catalog and advertising work, as well as highly publicized runway shows.

Finally, let's not forget that high fashion is not nearly as restricted as it used to be. It is now much more open to heights under five nine here and there, and unique-looking faces and bodies that never would have been considered for a modeling career in the past. I'm not trying to say it's easy to break into the modeling industry these days, but I am trying to tell you that many more avenues are open to you than before, because of both a shift in the public's way of looking at models, and the industry's acceptance of a more varied type of person to sell their high-fashion clothing or products.

In addition, promotional modeling has become a solid part of the marketing industry and provides an opportunity for people to start making money right away, while either trying their luck at fashion modeling, or just looking for some extra cash while trying to jump-start a career. Promotional modeling—which is also called "live" modeling, or "event staffing"—is the broadest area of modeling. It encompasses people of *all* age ranges and types and promotes a wide variety of products, from cars to liquor to television shows. I describe these very different categories later on in the book, and you will be able to decide what is more suitable for your type of look and personality as we move further along.

Marsha McMorrough, owner of the Diamond Agency in Orlando, Florida, where Mandy Moore started her career as a young girl, wholeheartedly agrees about the increased range of different types of models in the twenty-first century. She frequently books people ages forty to fifty, as well as senior citizens in their eighties! The newest craze that she has observed is agencies booking real-life families for jobs that need families to sell their product. One of her biggest clients is Walt Disney, and they routinely use families to advertise their international travel service, Adventures by Disney. Marsha also gets a lot of requests for real-life couples, and she explains that "people who are really together in their everyday life as a family, as opposed to separately chosen members of a family, have a certain natural chemistry that is hard to find otherwise. Also, when a client sends families on trips, the kids feel more comfortable with their real parents, plus, the client saves money by putting them all in the same room! It's a win-win situation." Log on to www.adventuresby disney.com and check out for yourself all of the various kinds of families they use. Families are now a rapidly growing part of the business! So you see how modeling ranges from one extreme to the other.

If you are in the central Florida area and have a good-looking family, send your pictures to the Diamond Agency! Their contact information is in the back of this book. Just remember, no need for professional photos, please. Wow—we aren't even through the introduction and I have already given some of you a valuable contact to utilize. Take advantage of it—and there is much more to come for all you other types as well.

Prepare Yourself for Rejection

We're almost ready to begin the four-step process, but I have to mention one more thing that is really important before we go on . . . you need to realize that unfortunately rejection (on a repetitive basis) is *completely unavoidable.* I don't care what you look like, or who you think you are or can be, someone is going to turn you down for something, and most likely it will happen again and again, because success in the modeling industry is not based on any objective criteria. There is no way to apply specific qualifications to being a successful model, as you can with careers that need certain degrees or licenses. Everyone who looks at you will see you in a different way, as it is only natural for every human being to see each person differently. And thank God for that—can you imagine if everyone saw you in the same way, day after day, and you could never change? We might as well all be robots, it would be so boring. Since the modeling industry is based on subjectivity, brace yourself for differences of opinion every time you start thinking you are "getting it." I am still "getting" things after twenty years in this business!

Since everyone is going to tell you different things about your looks, let their comments fly over your head if they are not saying what you want to hear. Please, do not take advice or criticism *too* seriously from just one person. Market yourself by spreading your wings and getting advice from as many sources as you can, so you can make informed conclusions or decisions about your career.

I am warning you about rejection early on, because even before you start the first part of chapter 1, you need to know how commonplace it is. I mention it throughout the book, but you *will* learn how to turn it around to your advantage by the time it starts happening. I will teach you how to take a comment from an industry professional and figure out if it is constructive, or if he or she is just looking for a way to get you out the door. But to do this objectively, you must have a thick skin and take everything that everyone says analytically, and not personally. By learning from the rejection and criticism, you can make yourself a better candidate for future evaluations of yourself. That's what modeling is: constant improvement and evaluation on the whole self, of which the product is YOU.

Learn, Learn, Learn

Whether you want to model as a hobby, or you would like eventually to be full-time, the four Ps I have created for you are the best way to get into the business. They are also the standard for being successful in the industry once you get an agency. It is crucial that you also know other information as well, such as scams, business advice, and many other tips. There are so many facets of the modeling industry to learn, and by condensing the most important ones for you, I hope to guide you in the best manner that I possibly can.

Preparation is the most important step for you to begin the process of developing a modeling career. So many people just jump straight into paying for worthless pictures, showing up at modeling agency open calls unprepared, or trying to market themselves to an agency that doesn't suit them. If they would have just taken the time to learn more about the industry and about how to ask the right questions, they could have saved a lot of time and money, as well as gotten responses from industry professionals that made more sense. The more you know, the better prepared you will be once you start getting those responses from agencies, whether the comments are negative or positive. It's all about evaluating yourself, then approaching the right people, so you can eventually market yourself in the area where you are meant to be. And the proper preparation puts you way ahead of the rest—which is where you have to be in such a fiercely competitive industry. Good luck, and I look forward to hearing plenty of success stories in the future!

PREPARATION

Strategic Marketing Is the Key

My whole philosophy on breaking into the modeling industry is based on a "target marketing" concept. There are endless geographical markets for you to explore, depending on where you live or where you are willing to move. Within those markets are hundreds of agencies, with thousands of agents working in those agencies, as well as managers and scouts, all of them looking for the next great face. You don't need to market yourself to *all* of those agencies; that would be a waste of time. More often than not, anyone looking to sign a model to an agency (such as an agent, a manager, or a scout) has a particular geographical area to search, or they simply live in the area where they work. So if *they* are being specific, why not you?

You will need to narrow down that search by figuring out specifically where you should be knocking on doors, and whom you should be trying to get to know for your kind of look as a model. It's certainly a much more efficient way to enter into the business as opposed to blindly sending pictures in to an agency, where the photos would probably get lost in the shuffle, sent to the wrong division, or thrown away without even being looked at. There is a definite strategy to not only reaching agents all over the world but also modifying your search so you are focused on agencies that are appropriate for your type of look.

The first chapter is divided into three parts to make the preparation process more understandable. I will briefly describe each part and then go into detail about how you will be utilizing each one.

1. categories of modeling
2. model identification
3. fitness

Teaching you the categories of modeling helps you start the process of "target marketing" yourself to the agencies, by narrowing down your scope. These categories are the way agencies are arranged, and in order to focus in on which division in an agency you should be aiming for specifically, you need to know about how the agencies are organized internally. Random mailings and mass e-mails to nonspecific divisions within agencies are a shot in the dark (at a tiny target).

The descriptions of the category titles are very specific and do not vary much from agency to agency. Some of the smaller agencies may not have as many divisions as others though. Please read these descriptions carefully, and get to know the way agencies are set up firsthand. Remember, knowledge is power! That's why you are reading this book in the first place—I have the answers that will help you break into the modeling industry.

Model identification is just that—identifying yourself as a certain type of model from the categories listed in this chapter. This will help you be even more specific in your search for an agency. You should "know" yourself inside and out, meaning: body type, personality, goals, and dreams. I am going to lead you on a "search for self" to make sure you are on the right track, and even more sure that you are trekking toward the appropriate goal when you start marketing yourself. A big mistake that potential models make is selling themselves to the wrong people! Finding the correct contacts for your type is easy, if you have the honesty to recognize what type you really are.

Finally, part three emphasizes the importance of fitness and eating a healthy diet. A lot of people think that models starve themselves to get skinny, but if you are savvy to the basics of nutrition, you will find that keeping fit is easier than you once thought. And by the way, being *too* skinny is not so in vogue anymore.

Categories of Modeling

The following categories are standard for all modeling agencies. There are a few agencies that will house all of these categories, which are usually called "divisions," but many agencies specialize in just a few of them, or sometimes only one. These categories are how the agencies split up their models and the models' agents (sometimes called "bookers" in the industry) to focus in on one particular type of modeling. As there are specific types of models, there are also specialized agents as well as model managers to mold a certain type of model's career. *Pay close attention* to the categories I list for you, because at the end of this segment I am going to have you pick one or two that you fall into.

I list the categories first by their name, and then next to the name I list what agencies (from my experience) often call this category within their company. These titles vary from agency to agency, and I certainly do not cover all of them. If you spot the term "board," it's just another word for "division" within an agency. Agencies often say they represent models on their different "boards." You can define this term as the corporate world does, "supervisory group," but you will find that in the modeling world the lingo tends to be more simplified than that. My theory for the reason behind the use of the term "board" instead of "division" is that in modeling agencies the old-fashioned "board" (as in wooden "board") was the circular desk that agents sat at to book the models, and before the days of computer technology, the paper charts of the models were in the middle on a lazy Susan so everyone could reach them. Pretty simple, right? As you learn the terms, you will see that nothing is too difficult to understand, and everyone tends to make things easy for new models entering the industry.

I will then list the demographic (age, etc.) and physical requirements (measurements), then a brief explanation of what that particular type of modeling is about. I go into further detail about all of these types of modeling later on in the book from a broader perspective, but for now, concentrate only on the category requirements. I also added sample model composites from select agencies that you may not have heard of but are still very good. These composites give you a glimpse of what you will eventually need to have as a working model. A "composite" is similar in its purpose to a business card, but with pictures. Measurements and your agency's contact information are on the back, although I mostly show only the *front* of these composites here. These composites have been chosen to show you the broad expanse that the modeling industry covers, as well as how diverse the selection of models can be. The composites are usually on card stock paper and vary slightly in size, but you will get the idea.

The categories for which I have not shown composites (runway, fit, and kids) were too extensive for me to begin to pick an example of that category. The two categories of runway and fit vary a lot from market to market, as far as the typical "look" of this category. Some fit models don't even have composites! The child modeling category, as you can imagine, encompasses endless possibilities of children from the age of a few months to eighteen years old.

The first seven categories are for women, the next four for men, and the last one is for children of both genders. I made sure to put the important points that I have to make about each division in both the male and female versions. Please read *all* of the descriptions for your gender, because I may mention something in one of them that pertains to everyone. After you are done reviewing all the categories thoroughly, I will teach you the remaining two parts of the preparation process.

Note: To reach any of the following modeling agencies or photographers, use their Web site and/or contact information listed in the back of this book. I purposely did not include composites from any of the larger agencies (like Ford, Elite, Next, IMG, etc.) because I felt that those agencies are easier to find when searching for modeling agencies on the Internet, and I wanted to expose you to other great agencies around the world.

WOMEN: HIGH FASHION NEW FACES
(OR DEVELOPMENT BOARD)

- Height: 5'8"–6' tall
- Dress size: 0–6
- Good skin and teeth
- Age: 13–22
- Measurements: 32AA–36B or C (bust), 22–26 inches (waist), 32–35.5 inches (hips)—very few high-fashion models these days get away with 36-inch hips

This is the high-end category for women and has very strict standards. If your measurements are even half an inch greater than any of these measurements, *wait* until they are within these criteria, or pick another category immediately. These women book the highest-profile magazines, advertising, campaigns, couture and high-end runway shows, and upscale catalogs.

The use of the term "high-fashion" as opposed to just "fashion" in the category title is the difference between young, trendy, and up-and-coming potential superstar models, and everyone else. The designers and magazines (often called "editorials"), as well as the stylists, hair and makeup artists, and photographers who work with these models are strictly of a higher-end caliber. The focus of the high-fashion modeling world is couture fashion, high-end campaigns, and the highly coveted cosmetic contract. A major cosmetic contract is the best paid job that you can get in the industry, as well as the most noteworthy, and it frequently adds up to several million dollars for only one or a few days of work at a time.

The high-fashion new-faces category only has room for a small percentage of people, and an even smaller portion actually make enough money to live comfortably. Just because you meet the qualifications listed here, there's no guarantee you will be able to model in that category. It only means that you have passed the most basic requirements to

Stang is one example of a female high-fashion new-faces model. Originally from Thailand, she started her career with me in New York City at E Model Management. At the age of fifteen, she was already six feet tall! Almost as soon as she arrived in New York, she was walking in fashion shows for top designers at New York's internationally acclaimed Fashion Week.
Photo: Alexey Yurenev

be in this category. If you fall within these criteria, great! You have passed the first step to *possibly* becoming a high-fashion model.

The next hurdle is finding that indescribable "look." If you have all of the requirements but not that "look" the agents talk about when a girl first walks into a room, then it does not matter if you fall within the criteria listed above. Agents have tried over and over again to describe that "look" or "feeling" they get when they see a model they would like to represent for possible superstardom. The only comparison I can think of is that it's kind of like when you see someone you have a crush on, and it seems to take your breath away for a moment. You just "feel it" when you see someone that is desirable, and instinct takes over. Models are looked at in much the same way by an agency, which is why personality is so important. As Ms. Samersova said in the introduction of this book, it's the "spirit" of a girl who walks in the room that counts the most in the end. You will hear me say repeatedly throughout this book that first impressions count, but that so-called feeling (if modeling agents get it about you) will be shot down if you do not fall within this category's physical requirements right from the start.

And yes, high-fashion agencies start looking for girls at the ages of twelve or thirteen years old. Don't cringe, Mom! She won't be packing her bags for Europe just yet. If a young girl is at or close to the minimum height at this age and has a great face, she will be considered as a potential high-fashion model, and the agency or manager that takes her on will wait until she is either mature enough to handle a photo shoot, tall enough to be the minimum height, or until the parents are ready to make a commitment one way or the other. If a girl is an inch or two shy of the five-eight minimum and she is not yet fifteen years old, then sometimes agencies or managers will want to sign her on anyway, with the belief that she will grow in the next year or two. More detailed advice for parents is written toward the end of this book (along with the difference between managers and agents), but I will tell you here that anyone trying to pressure Mom or Dad into paying for anything (especially at that age) is not a legitimate representative of the modeling industry. There is *no rush* at that age for anything, and the girl and her parents should be treated with patience and a regard for her potential.

A model in this category could go years without making a profit, then all of a sudden—BAM! She hits it big and is the most wanted face in the world. Later on in this book I will explain both why this is so and the process a high-fashion new-faces model goes through. This category is also the most competitive, which you probably already realized.

If you are considering trying to break into this category, do your research! Read the high-fashion magazines, take note of who the photographers and models are in the fashion stories, watch Fashion

Television and see how the models posture themselves, and log on to www.models.com for the latest news from modeling agencies around the world. *Become a high-fashion model inside your head—visualize your career.* Having a passion for what you do is most important, and to know a lot about the business you are getting into is always a great advantage when trying to sell yourself to others.

WOMEN: HIGH FASHION
(ALSO MAIN FASHION OR HIGH BOARD)

- Height: 5'8"–6' tall
- Dress size: 0–6
- Age: 18–29
- Measurements: 32AA–36C (bust), 22–27 inches (waist), 32–36.5 inches (hips)

This category is for the more mature female who is in her twenties (who *reads* age eighteen to around thirty-five or so—you don't actually have to be twenty-nine years old to *look* twenty-nine) who is not a candidate for a new-faces division in a high-fashion modeling agency, because of age, or who has already tried the new-faces division and did not become a celebrity or a campaign girl. It is a more forgiving area than a new-faces division, because the requirements are a *little* broader. Don't get me wrong, it's still not easy to break into, but you have more of a chance with this one.

Agencies will look for new girls in this category who demonstrate a stronger, more confident look (like a girl who has a more mature face than most teenagers do), or if a model was in a new-faces division of a high-fashion agency already and is either older or is not getting as much work in new faces as they once were. This category also considers models if they have some experience behind them, either from another market, or in other types of modeling work. In New York, it is easier to break into the main fashion category if you have a portfolio

This is Jenny Molin, from the women's high-fashion division of
Model Team Agency, located in Hamburg, Germany. She is
one of Model Team's top moneymaking girls on an international
scale.
Photo: Signe Vilstrup

that an agency has helped you to obtain and you come from a secondary market. A secondary market is a city that is smaller and has a different level of competition than a city such as New York or Los Angeles.
Examples of secondary markets would be Chicago, Dallas, or Philadelphia. An agency in New York probably won't use one picture that is in
your portfolio when you get to New York from a secondary market,
but they will consider the experience an advantage. And of course,
main fashion divisions will take on beginning models as well.

WOMEN: SOPHISTICATED FASHION (OR CLASSIC)

- Height: 5'8"–6' tall
- Dress size: 0–8
- Age: 30 and up

This division is an offshoot of the women's main division, a category in which a female can be considered to be a "young mother" or at an age when she can advertise "wrinkle cream." This category can also include celebrities who are older campaign girls. I did not put specific measurements in the requirements this time, just dress sizes, because as a model gets older, the measurements become more forgiving.

Notice that the word "high" is not part of this category's name. It's a little confusing because "high-fashion" modeling agencies sometimes have other divisions that are not "high fashion." This doesn't necessarily mean these girls do not work with high-end designers. It means that the work they do is on a different level—and even though it's not such a high-profile division, females can still do very well financially here. Sometimes a model in the high-fashion division (which is higher-profile work) is forced to accept a high-caliber job for very little or no money, just to get her face out to the public, or for the opportunity to work with a famous photographer or stylist. Models in general (especially high-fashion models) do not make a lot of money all of the time, despite what the media often insinuates.

There is more commercial-type work in this category ("commercial" meaning more mainstream, not television commercials), as opposed to the more edgy high-fashion category, and the editorial starts changing from magazines like *Elle* and *Cosmopolitan* to magazines for a more mature readership, such as *More* and *Family Circle*. Each category has clients that are more suitable to the genre they represent, and older women simply market products for, well, older women. Don't laugh—being over thirty in the fashion industry is considered to be "old." Sorry!

Karen Howard is a great example of a model belonging to a women's classic division. From North Carolina, she has a box full of numerous *Vogue* and *Harper's Bazaar* covers from her career as a high-fashion model, and she is now a model with Directions USA in Greensboro, North Carolina.
Photo: Fadil Berisha

WOMEN: COMMERCIAL PRINT (OR LIFESTYLE)

- Height: 5′2″–6′ tall
- Dress size: 0–10
- Nice smile
- Age: 18–80

Models in this category do not need previous modeling experience (in other words, tear sheets from magazines, etc.). Sometimes

Laura Martin is a commercial print model with Bella
Agency in New York City. She is a perfect example
of a gorgeous female model who is in the
commercial print world (as opposed to "high
fashion").
Photo: David Kaptein

models who do not work enough in either high fashion or for the
catalog world (main fashion) will try this category. Commercial print
is geared more to "product" advertising as opposed to "fashion" advertising (for example, modeling to sell laundry detergent, as opposed
to gowns worn on the red carpet). It's not that these models aren't
"pretty"; they just don't need to be up to the typical high-fashion standard. The few exceptions of more moderately priced catalogs that the
agencies work with would be for stores such as Kmart, JCPenney,
and Sears.

Commercial print models will often be put in real-life situations to model a product, instead of having photo shoots in a studio with a white wall or a trendy, funky setup, which is more common with high-fashion modeling.

Hint: There are some very strong commercial print divisions within select commercial and television agencies! A large number of "talent" agencies have commercial print modeling divisions because they go hand in hand. The marketing process for you is the same, even though a television agency is not a "fashion" agency. Do not be misled by the word "talent" in the name of an agency. Also, some of the high-fashion agencies have commercial print divisions too, like Ford Models in New York. You just have to do your research to find out which ones do both.

WOMEN: RUNWAY (OR SHOWROOM)

- Height: 5'7"–6' tall
- Dress size: 0–8
- Age: 17 and up

These models usually are more mainstream models who do not have as strong a career in the print world. A model working runway or showroom clients will work wherever her measurements are applicable. These models go to the clients' offices, trade shows, or showrooms to work. Sometimes an agency will combine fitting work (which is described in the next category) with this category as well. The runway jobs for models vary, ranging from press events to actual mini runway shows for their clients.

This category should not be confused with the high-fashion shows during the modeling industry's fashion show season. "Show models" are the high-fashion models that strut down the runway for the couture or trendy up-and-coming designers and are currently in high-profile international fashion magazines. The models found in these shows are usually with a high-fashion new-faces division, and many are with the main division within an agency as well. These are the shows with heavy press coverage that celebrities attend. Fashion show season is a big deal in the modeling industry and is held twice a year all over the world, and once a year in some of the smaller markets and countries. The cities that are the most sought after for fashion show season are New York, Paris, London, and Milan. Los Angeles just recently began its own show circuit, along with the Caribbean and Miami Beach. If you want a complete list of shows around the world, go onto www.lerage.com, and you can see the different countries that hold them, along with pictures of the models who walked the runways.

Do not be fooled by this category, or the next one, which is "Fit." Many models are making well over $100,000 a year in these categories. There are a lot of "repeat" clients in this area, which means they use the same girls over and over again. Once you get in with a client, you could have a steady job for a long period of time. I used to represent a model who got paid $2,000 a day for *one* showroom client, and she worked about seventy-five days a year for them. *One client!* This can be quite a lucrative area, even though it is behind the scenes at a designer's corporate office or showroom. And you do not need a lot of experience to work as a showroom model, unlike someone in high-fashion modeling, who typically needs tear sheets from magazines in their portfolio or simply great pictures.

WOMEN: FITTINGS (OR FIT)

- Heights and sizes vary
- Age: 16–60

Typical clients for this category are huge corporations like Ralph Lauren, Gap, or Talbots who need specific sizes for their designers as a starting point to make a complete range of sizes of clothing that will eventually be sold in their stores. Fit models range from petite to plus sizes, but the most in demand is size eight. If your height is five seven to five eight, your bust is 36B (35½ inches), waist is 28 inches, and your hips are 38½ inches, you could make a lot of money going to offices where clothing lines are put together to fit the clothing on a regular basis. There *is* work for men as well, but it is limited.

But there are also many other measurements in demand (including plus size and petite), and to find out whether or not you have what it takes, you need to send your pictures to an agency that has a division such as this, or that specializes in this type of modeling such as Fit, LLC in New York City.

The fit category does not have aesthetic requirements, except that the model is "presentable." For instance, the model should have an easygoing personality and a clean-cut appearance (no tattoos, piercings, etc.). They especially like girls with personality, because a client will use a fit model for several hours at a time, pinning her clothes, trying things on, and taking Polaroids, and the model must be patient. It's even better if she has a sense of humor!

You could have almost *any* kind of look, especially for fit modeling, so go for it! I am banking on the fact that you are not trying to break into the modeling business if you think you are ugly.

Note: I included this category in my list because several modeling agencies have this division and there are also agencies that book only fit work, but you can also break into it *without* an agency. A more detailed section on fit models is included on page 38.

WOMEN: PLUS SIZE

- Height: 5'8"–6'
- Dress size: 10–24
- Age: 16–60
- Proportional figure—evenly distributed curves
- Good skin and teeth

This category title is self-explanatory; these women can work in the same jobs mentioned in the women's high-fashion category, with jobs pertaining to catalog, advertising, and advertising campaigns, fittings,

BECCA

This is Becca, from Nova Models located in Baltimore, Maryland. Notice that her composite is not strictly a head shot—sometimes the model or her agency chooses to be a bit different in creating a composite, so it has more of a chance to get noticed.
Photo: Stanley Debas

showroom, and fashion shows for clients such as Lane Bryant. This category has been quickly growing in popularity for the past six or seven years, and there is more and more work available for plus-size models. Larger agencies are more likely to have a plus-size division, and there are a few agencies that specialize in plus-size modeling. Size ten is on the smaller side for this category, as there is not as much work for a size ten model, but it also depends on your bone structure. If your face is wide and your body is larger framed, size ten could be an option. Your bust, waist, and hip measurements should generally be ten inches away from each other to create the look of a more evenly distributed figure. There *is* work for sizes larger than twenty, but not as much.

MEN: HIGH FASHION NEW FACES
(OR DEVELOPMENT)

- Height: 5'11½"–6'2½"
- Suit size: 38–42L
- Waist: 28–34 inches
- Nice teeth, good skin, prominent jawbone
- Age: 17–25

This is the men's high-end category, and it demands very strict standards. If your sizes do not fit these requirements, *wait* until they do. High-fashion male models book magazines, advertising campaigns, couture and high-end runway shows, and upscale catalogs.

The use of the term "high fashion" as opposed to just "fashion" is the difference between young, trendy, and up-and-coming superstar models, and everyone else. As with women, the designers and magazines (often called "editorials") as well as the stylists, hair and makeup artists, and photographers who work with these male models are strictly of a higher-end caliber.

Fitness is more closely scrutinized for male models as opposed to female, especially in high fashion. Where a female model can get away with just having the correct measurements, male models have to have more of a defined physique. Here's where that six-pack comes in handy, and it's not the one in your refrigerator! You will have more of an advantage the more defined your muscles are, but don't go too overboard, designers don't like muscles to overpower their clothing. Clothing tends to drape better on men who are fit, but don't be too bulky in the shoulders, chest, or legs.

This high-fashion arena includes only a small percentage of the population, and an even smaller percent actually make enough money to live comfortably. Just because you meet the qualifications listed for

Matt Rogers is a male model in the new-faces
division of Directions USA Agency in North
Carolina. Matt's composite is in black and white,
which is sometimes more creatively appealing for
the high-fashion clients.
Photo: Ron Reagan

high fashion, that does not guarantee you will be able to model in that
category. It just means you have passed the first hurdle.

The indescribable "look" also comes into play here. If you have all
of the specifications but not that "look" the agents talk about when a
guy first walks in the room, then it does not matter that you fall within
these criteria. Agents have tried over and over again to describe the
"feeling" that comes when they see a model they would like to represent, and it's kind of like trying to describe how you feel when you see
a hot girl (or guy, depending on your preference). You just "feel it"
when you see that person, and instinct takes over. You will hear me say
repeatedly throughout this book that first impressions count, but even
if the agents get that so-called feeling about you, you will be shot

down if you do not fall within this category's requirements right from the beginning.

A model in this category could go years without making a profit, then all of a sudden—BAM! He hits it big and is the most wanted face in the world. Later on in this book I will explain both why this is so and the process a high-fashion new-faces model goes through. This category is also the most competitive, which you probably already realized.

If you are considering trying to break into this category, do your research! Read the high-fashion magazines for men, note who the photographers and models are in the fashion stories, watch Fashion Television and see how the models posture themselves, and log on to www.models.com for the latest news from modeling agencies around the world. *Become a high-fashion model inside your head—visualize your career.* Having a passion for what you do is most important, and to know a lot about the business you are getting into is always a great advantage when trying to sell yourself to others.

MEN: HIGH FASHION
(OR MAIN FASHION OR HIGH BOARD)

- Height: 5'11½"–6'2½"
- Suit size: 38–42L
- Waist: 28–34 inches
- Nice teeth, good skin, prominent jawbone
- Age: 17–30

This category is for the more mature male who *reads* ages seventeen to thirty-five. You don't actually have to be thirty years old to be able to *look* thirty years old. This category is appropriate for a model who is not a candidate, because of his age, for a new-faces division in a high-fashion modeling agency, or who has already tried new faces and not become a supermodel or campaign model. It is a more forgiving area than the new-faces category, because the requirements are a bit broader. Don't get

THE campbell
3906 lemmon ave. suite 200
dallas, tx 75219
tel. 214.522.8991
AGENCYfax. 214.522.8997

TREY
SINGLETON

Based in Dallas, Trey Singleton is a high-fashion male
model from the Campbell Agency who is getting more
and more work as he heads into his thirties. There are
catalogs—including those for JCPenney, Dillard's, and
Foley's—that are based in the Southwest. For a model
living in that area, such work could be quite lucrative.
Photo: Scott Teitler

me wrong, it's still not easy to break into, but you have more of a chance
with this one.

Agencies will look for new faces in this category that demonstrate a
stronger, more confident look (like a man who has a more mature face
than most teenagers do), or if a model was in a new-faces division of a
high-fashion agency already and is either older or is not getting as much
work in new faces as they once were. This category also considers models

if they have some experience behind them, either from another market, or in other types of modeling work. In New York, it is easier to break into the main fashion category if you have a portfolio that an agency has helped you to obtain and you come from a secondary market. A secondary market is a city that is smaller and has a different level of competition than a city such as New York or Los Angeles. Examples of secondary markets would be Chicago, Dallas, or Philadelphia. An agency in New York probably won't use one picture that is in your portfolio when you get to New York, but they will consider the experience an advantage. And of course, main fashion divisions will take on beginning models as well.

MEN: SOPHISTICATED FASHION (OR CLASSIC)

- Height: 5'11"–6'2½"
- Suit size: 38–44L
- Waist: 28–34 inches
- Nice teeth, good skin, prominent jawbone
- Age: 30 and up

The requirements are basically the same as the high-fashion men (the suit size is a little more forgiving), but the ages go from around thirty years to about fifty, in some cases even older. This category is for "older" men who are more commercial, have a more mature look, or who had formerly been in a high-fashion division but are now developing an older appeal. This age group might sell hair color for gray hair, or do Father's Day advertising for department stores and such. A nice bonus for this category is that men can be older than women as a new face (it isn't as strict for age), and older male models have much more of a chance at a longer career than female models do.

Notice that the word "high" is not part of this category's name. It's a little confusing because "high-fashion" modeling agencies sometimes have other divisions that are not "high fashion." This doesn't necessarily

TOM CLARK

Tom Clark is a sophisticated male model who exemplifies the classic male model look. Clark works with the Diamond Agency in Orlando, Florida. His head shot shows a friendly, warm personality along with classic features and a great smile.
Photo: Lou Freeman

mean these men do not work with high-end designers. It means that the work they do is on a different level—and even though it's not such a high-profile division, males can still do very well financially here. Sometimes a model in the high-fashion division (which is higher-profile work) is forced to accept a high-caliber job for very little or no money, just to get his face out to the public, or for the opportunity to work with a famous photographer or stylist. Models in general (especially high-fashion models) do not make a lot of money all the time, despite what the media often insinuates.

Hair: Salt & Pepper
Eyes: Blue
Height: 6'1"
Suit: 40R
Waist: 32
Neck: 15 1/2
Sleeve: 34
Inseam: 32
Shoe: 11-d
Sweater: Med.
Hand Model
Glove: 9 1/2
Ring: 10 1/4
SAG & AFTRA
Extensive Wardrobe

Jed Todd
Greer Lange Model & Talent Agency
610-747-0300
www.GreerLange.com

Jed Todd is a male commercial print model with
salt-and-pepper hair, from the Greer Lange Model and
Talent Agency in Philadelphia, Pennsylvania. This full-length
shot can be described as more "lifestyle," set in a more
casual scene—almost as though Jed did not know the
camera was there. But at the same time this shot shows off
his facial bone structure.
Photo: Floyd M. Dean

MEN: COMMERCIAL PRINT (OR LIFESTYLE)

- Height: 5'8"–6'3"
- Clean-cut appearance
- Nice teeth and good skin

- Evenly proportioned body, relatively fit
- Age: 18 and up

Models in this category do not need previous modeling experience (in other words, tear sheets from magazines, etc.). Some of the high-fashion agencies have a commercial print division and some do not. Other modeling agencies only book commercial print. Sometimes models who do not do enough work in either high fashion or for the catalog world (main fashion) will try this category. Commercial print is geared more to "product" advertising as opposed to "fashion" catalogs or advertising (for example, modeling to sell a computer as opposed to a tuxedo). It's not that these models aren't "handsome"; they just don't need to be up to the typical high-fashion standard. The few exceptions of more moderately priced catalogs that the agencies work with would be for stores such as Kmart, JCPenney, and Sears.

Hint: There are some very strong commercial print divisions within select commercial and television agencies! A large number of "talent" agencies have commercial print modeling divisions because they go hand in hand. The marketing process for you is the same even though a television agency is not a "fashion" agency. Do not be misled by the word "talent" in the name of an agency. Also, some of the high-fashion agencies have commercial print divisions too, like Ford Models in New York. You just have to do your research to find out which ones do both.

KIDS

- Age: babies to 18 years old
- Bold, friendly personalities
- Clear skin
- Beautiful smiles

All parents think their child is beautiful. But unless you want professional shots in your family's photo album, do not waste money on professional pictures of them—children change so much as they grow and their looks shift so rapidly, professional photos will quickly be outdated. They are simply not worth the cost. Once a child is signed by an agency, the agency will help to get professional pictures, but not before a child is a certain age.

Select modeling agencies will represent toddlers and babies. Not everyone will take preschool-age kids or babies, so you have to find out from each particular agency what ages they represent before you choose to send pictures to them.

Many *acting* agencies do not start kids until they are four years old. It is a smart move to try to get a commercial agent along with a print agent if your child is old enough, because your child's chances for work will increase if you can get him or her a modeling *and* an acting agency. The whole process of marketing is the same. If the child is over four years old and looking for commercial representation, then that child should be able to be in a room with an agent without the parents, and listen to instruction well. This standard rule also applies to when a child is going on commercial *castings,* because a modeling agency will sometimes get commercial auditions as well, and kids have to be willing to go into an audition by themselves and listen to the casting director. I go into more detail about warnings and tips for child modeling and acting in chapter 7, under the section "A Word to Parents."

I did not include a picture of a typical child model for these reasons: (1) Kids' agencies normally do not use professional pictures or composites, so I would be putting in a family photo, which I think is silly. (2) I couldn't think of a reason not to put *my* kids' picture in this book over all the others! And that did not seem fair to you, the reader.

Not Just for Tall, Skinny People Anymore

You have probably noticed that most of these categories are for taller people. Within the industry, designers have always leaned toward tall and thin. But nowadays, that is not always the case. Kate

Moss broke the rules for the typical model being at least five nine (even five eight!), and Emme started the plus-size rave by not being the typical size four to six. The commercial print height requirement starts drastically lower than high fashion, with a minimum height requirement of five two. Why? Unlike couture designers, who sell fashions and want their models to be tall, this category sells products. Corporations selling household products or electronics, for instance, mostly sell their products with models who are more average in height *and* size. The Chanel girl who is tall and skinny and perfect for couture gowns is not necessarily the same image that Pampers diapers wants to portray to new mothers. The product or fashion needs not only to fit the look of the model but also to be able to reach out to the proper audience. Read on folks, and you will not only learn about modeling, but marketing and advertising as well!

FIT MODELING

Fit modeling is the most unique (in my opinion) form of modeling that there is. The term "fit" means that the models in this category try on the clothing to see how it fits for a particular designer or department store. This type of modeling uses all heights and sizes, from petite to plus sizes, and that by itself is astounding. But being a fit model entails so much more than just looking good—the most experienced fit models are known as "technical consultants," such as Helen Powers, who has been fit modeling for *thirty* years and has made upward of $300,000 a year for multiple years in a row. Helen began her career after working in a showroom part time and scanning the *Women's Wear Daily* (otherwise known as *WWD*) for fit model castings. She then made additional contacts from those bookings and eventually got representation at an agency that had a fit division. (Helen suggests that another way to research on your own for casting calls in fit modeling is on the Web site Craig's List at www.craigslist.com.)

A retail background helps if you are targeting the fit modeling industry, because this type of model not only models the clothing but also works closely with the designer to put together an outfit for the mass public. Helen said that it's important to learn the "technicalities and construction of a garment," because "the clients will rely on my expertise for their manufacturing." Fit modeling can be extremely technical! And an experienced fit model needs to understand fully how to describe the proper fit for each piece of clothing to a client or designer.

Fit modeling sometimes is compared to showroom modeling, where the modeling is more "runway" type of work, although there is a significant difference in the *communication* between the client and model in fit and showroom modeling. With fit modeling, the model is being constantly asked how the garment fits, what the difference is in fabric, etc., while showroom modeling is more "mannequin" modeling, where there is not so much interaction with the designers, and the model does not have to know any garment industry lingo or about how the fabrics are made.

Helen told me that she and a few other fit models that she knows who work all the time don't even *use* composites or need portfolios. She has even done fittings over the Web cam for clients in Europe, so with the help of technology, her career is not limited to the United States. But although Web cams reach her international clients, Helen has also traveled extensively in her career as a fit model, so a career in fit modeling definitely does not limit you to the area in which you start. This unique type of modeling should be considered closely because of its lucrative salary potential.

Helen emphasizes that "you don't have to be beautiful! Just have a positive personality, and knowledge of clothing and the way it's put together to help you get started." I tested out the waters myself and searched on Craig's List for national opportunities in fit modeling. Clients all over the United States are looking for fit models, one example being a sportswear company looking for a fit model who is 5'5½", dress size twelve, in Boulder, Colorado, with "communication" skills. So you see? The range is endless, you just have to do your research. As an extra plus in your favor, familiarize yourself with sewing lingo so you'll have an edge on other people applying for the job. Go onto Helen's Web site to learn more about what it's like to actually be a fit model: www.helenpowers.com. Click on her video done by CNN and you can even see her live at work to give you more of an idea of what a fit model does.

PROMOTIONAL MODELING

- Age: 18 and up
- Heights and sizes vary
- Good skin
- Nice white, straight teeth
- Body in good condition
- Friendly and warm personality with a flair for sales
- No visible tattoos

Promotional modeling has become popular only within the past few years. This is a good way to earn money while trying to break into the "fashion print work" part of the business. These models do mostly "live" modeling, where they will stand around and promote various products. This category will mostly entail working at trade shows, shopping malls, and some restaurants and nightclubs.

Since this is a new facet of the modeling world that hasn't been around for a long time or become very well known yet, I thought I would let you in on a few things I have discovered about the promotional modeling world.

In the age of digital technology, huge corporations are turning toward a type of market that is known as "event marketing" or "experiential marketing" to sell their products. Research has shown that it can be highly effective for consumers to touch, smell, or taste a product they are considering buying (to have a personal experience with the brand), as opposed to just staring at it on a piece of paper in a newspaper or magazine, or driving by a billboard at sixty miles an hour on a highway. Even more persuasive is if the customer gets a free sample to bring home! Whether it be a hundred people standing in the middle of Times Square in New York City passing out samples, or two people walking around in selected outfits at a clothing manufacturer's trade show, the effect is a more intimate way of marketing a chosen product. Some events are even staffed with promotional models called "product specialists" or "brand ambassadors" who are pretrained, so they can answer questions from the consumer more efficiently.

I was quite surprised when I found out that event marketing was a $171 billion industry! Promotional models get hired to do all sorts of events, including trade shows, conventions, street marketing, product launches, and more. The rate varies from twelve to sixty dollars per hour, usually for a minimum of four hours, and a maximum of six months or more. Most jobs vary from one to seven days, but there are promotional tours that go around the country for extended periods of time as well.

Here is the best part—not only do you *not* need professional pictures to get into this industry, but you also don't need them to *stay* in this industry! You can even register online for *free—and sit back and let the booking requests for your type roll into your e-mail box*. I did it myself and was shocked at the number of opportunities I was sent. You can pick and choose what jobs you want to submit yourself for, but be careful—when you get hired you must show up on time and be professional. Some people make the mistake of thinking no one will notice irresponsibility, especially when hundreds of people are working one job, but promotional agencies keep track of your every move. Some companies have computer files on everyone who signs up, with ratings on every model that works for them, so if they get a complaint about a certain model not showing up or being irresponsible, it is inputted into the system so that they can see who is doing their job effectively, and who is not. And if someone gets a low rating, that person will not get the next job. Heather Preston, senior staffing coordinator at GC Marketing Group, an event staffing company in New York City, says it perfectly: "One of the most important things to remember in [the promotional] business is networking and getting your name positively out there. People often forget this simple yet vital aspect of the business, to be your own PR first and foremost. It is detrimental to burn bridges, and even in an industry with such a large talent pool, staffing professionals will remember those who do not return phone calls or show up to jobs late, or who do not show up at all."

Founded by Gilad Carni, GC Marketing Group is a nationwide New York City–based promotional modeling staffing agency that hires promotional models for global advertising agencies, public relations companies, and event marketing firms. They have *over 15,000* people in their database so far. All you have to do is register online—it's *that easy*! And the fact that they are based in New York City does not mean most of their work is in New York—quite the opposite. While 30 percent of their business is booked in New York, a whopping 70 percent is booked across the country.

Promotional modeling is an excellent way to make extra cash while you are trying to break into the modeling business or even as a way to supplement your modeling salary. There are no registration fees, no percentages taken out, and no professional pictures needed. GC Marketing is one of many companies that staff promotional models, and to register on their Web site go to: www.gcmarketingservices.com. Photos are requested when you register and family pictures are fine, but here is where you can utilize your talents for picture taking in the way that I am going to show you. Your special nonprofessional pictures, which you will learn how to take in chapter 2, will *definitely* make you stand out next to someone who has not gone through the steps in this book. Working another job while trying to break into the modeling industry is a smart idea, and promotional modeling has flexible hours too. You may even want to continue a part-time job or promotional modeling at first even if you get representation right away because it tends to take a while for new models to start making a profit.

Promotional modeling is not officially considered "fashion modeling" by the modeling industry in general and should not be used to break into the fashion industry. Only "promotional modeling" agencies are interested in hearing that you have had experience with promotional work—it is totally separate from high fashion and commercial print work.

Now that you have been through the preparation steps, let's review all the category titles.

Women's High Fashion—New Faces
Women's High Fashion—High Board
Women's Sophisticated
Women's Commercial Print

Runway (women only)

Fit (women only)

Plus Size (women only)

Men's High Fashion—New Faces

Men's High Fashion—High Board

Men's Sophisticated

Men's Commercial Print

Kids

It may not hit you immediately which category or categories you are going to fall under, so start by measuring yourself first, to help you narrow down your options physically. The next section will help you with that, and how to correctly pinpoint yourself as a model "type," by zeroing in on your expectations versus reality in the modeling world. Once you actually review your measurements and figure out exactly what is appropriate for you, you may not have as many options as you originally thought you would have from the category list.

Model Identification

The first rule in identifying yourself as a model is to *be honest*! As you read through this section, I will explain to you how vitally important it is to be up front with yourself as a person *and* as a model from the very beginning. If I had a penny for each time during the past decade that a girl or guy gave me a size number or measurement incorrectly, I would be a millionaire. There are the people who exaggerate numbers slightly in their favor, the ones who are in denial about the numbers being correct on a tape measure, and those who are out-and-out boldface liars and think lying is going to get them ahead, that no one will notice an inch here and there. I have met them all! And so has every agent, scout, and manager in the modeling industry. If you go through this whole process in denial about your measurements or what modeling in general is like, you will not get the most out of this book.

Have you ever had someone come up to you and say you look exactly like a certain celebrity, and try as you might, you just can't see it?

My point is that people looking at you for potential model representation will most likely see you differently from how you see yourself. So please, try to put all your preconceived notions aside about what you perceive yourself to look like (especially when it comes to your measurements) and just objectively read what this business is about, and what you can do to make the right choices for yourself. I have broken this section up into two parts: the "physical" and the "mental" parts. The physical part is the one where you measure your physique. The mental part is where you look inside yourself and figure out where your head is at, as far as your goals and expectations are concerned.

Let's start with the physical. Measure yourself *before* declaring your numerical sizes. You may be surprised at what you *think* your measurements are. Better yet, get a friend to measure you so there is no cheating. Here is one very important tip: If you are female and you *think* your hips are 35 inches and they are really 36½ inches after measuring yourself and you selected the high-fashion category, you need to either slim down or switch to another category that is more appropriate for your size. Again—be honest with yourself, or this whole process will not work. I'm trying to save you some embarrassment—the agents *will* measure you themselves if they are interested, and the truth *will* come out!

Having already worked at several different high-fashion modeling agencies, I have seen dozens of girls come into town from overseas or wherever their home base is only to realize that the girl lied about her measurements, or gained enough weight so that she is a totally different size by the time she lands in New York City. Now, these girls had already signed a contract with whatever agency I was working with at the time, and we would send them right back to where they came from. Modeling agencies do not have time to waste on liars! If you have ever been in an agency (especially in New York City), there is barely time for the agent to get up from his or her chair to meet you, let alone spend time on a girl who thinks she is a size four when in reality she is a size eight. If you are not signed with an agency yet, it only looks worse, because it spoils the first impression, and you may not get a second chance with them. So you get my point—please be truthful about everything from the start! It will only benefit you in the end.

FOR MEN ONLY

As the plus-size modeling industry for women has grown, so has the overall male model population in the fashion industry. The popularity of male modeling has increased dramatically in the past decade. Male models do everything females do, just the male version. It's also one of the only industries that pays males less than females—sorry guys! But I don't have much sympathy for you when "less money" means that a day rate for an average catalog job starts at $1,500 a day. The rules are all the same as far as marketing yourself and staying fit. Some say that it is the only business where females get paid more than males on the whole, but male models, if they snag consistent work, in the long run can have a much longer career than females.

It is vitally important to determine what genre you fall into. By leafing through men's fashion magazines, you can quickly assess that male models have a wide range of looks, from grungy to clean-cut, and you need to figure out what works for you. Go through advertisements in magazines and look at different types of male models . . . are you more of a "Ralph Lauren" type of guy? Or are you ruggedly handsome, like the Marlboro man? Or do you fall into the romantic-looking category like the male models on the covers of romance novels? You need to do your research just like the women—there are some very macho magazines out there, so don't be embarrassed to look. *GQ, Esquire,* and *Men's Health* are all solid magazines that women usually never pick up, so you won't have to compromise your tough-guy image by reading one of these in public.

The reason I am asking you to do research before you go on is because I want you to find a look and stick with it. For example, long hair versus short hair and shaven versus unshaven are two totally different looks. Please do not take Polaroids or digital pictures of yourself shaven *and* unshaven to market to agencies—market yourself as one entity and *go for it!* Then, if you are not getting the response you want, take all the pictures over again with or without that facial hair. If you do not stay within a certain look when marketing yourself, you will only confuse anyone looking at your pictures and in the meantime will lose your identity as a model. Having a clear picture of what type of model you are and want to be is crucial to your marketing strategy. *Visualize* yourself as a certain kind of model and go after it with a wholehearted conviction.

TIPS ON MEASURING YOURSELF CORRECTLY

Here are some instructions on how to get the most accurate measurements that you can. Men will only need a waist measurement and a suit size for now. When you join an agency more detailed measurements will be taken at that time.

Please remember, don't suck in your stomach while measuring your waist or stand on your toes when determining your height. The truer the measurements you can get, the better!

- Put on a bikini for the girls; guys should don a pair of boxers or a swimsuit.
- Hold the measuring tape snug, but not tight.
- Make sure the tape is straight in the front and back.
- Measure your bust across the nipple area. (Men do not need this one.)
- Measure your waist where it curves in on both sides for the women, and right below the belly button for the men.
- Measure your hips at the fullest part, right above the groin area. (Men do not need this one either.)

You are not allowed to round off to the next lowest number or round up to the next highest in your height. That's why the industry uses "½" inches in their stat records! You're lucky—Europe uses the metric system, so there is almost no wiggle room there.

Also do not write a lower number down on the pictures that you are going to mail to the modeling agencies, thinking you are going to lose weight by the time anyone sees you in person. *Wait* until you are the actual measurement you desire. What happens if an agency calls you in before you expect it? Then you are seen as a liar, or even worse, desperate to be a model. Desperation is the worst impression to give when you are trying to find representation, and it all seems to start with people exaggerating about their measurements.

WHAT KIND OF MODEL YOU THINK YOU ARE

Now get ready for the thinking part. Selecting a category is not only about your measurements and sizes. You also need to take into consideration the job description of the category you selected. Think closely about the descriptions I have given you of the different areas of modeling such as high fashion, commercial print, showroom, fit, and promotional. What you *think* is involved in a certain category may be far from the truth of what that category actually requires in the working world. Try to set aside for a moment what you imagine life as a model to be. You may be surprised at how different the everyday life of a model actually is.

There are plenty of myths associated with the fashion industry. One of them is that you can live wherever you want, and another one is that models have a glamorous lifestyle all the time, wherever they live. Wrong! Unless you are already a supermodel, models *have* to go wherever the work is, and they need to be able to adapt to whatever their particular look requires. For example, when I first started modeling, my agent told me to cut off my hair and go to Italy. Well, I wanted my hair more than I wanted to model, plus, I had a boyfriend in the States who did not want to live abroad. So needless to say I hardly worked at all for the first two years because I had long hair and wouldn't move anywhere to further my career.

Then I decided to stop being so stubborn and start assuming my agent knew best. I realized I wasn't going to be the next Cindy Crawford (who was *the* supermodel of the decade when I was modeling), so I finally decided to cut my hair from past my shoulders up to my chin. The shorter my hair got, the more money I made, until I had *super* short hair, and I was working like crazy! I was ecstatic and enjoying a successful modeling career in Italy (by then I had moved there), and shot frequently for major magazines and campaigns out of Milan. I finally gave in to the things that I was trying to resist all along, and it helped me grow not only as a person but also as a model, besides being considerably profitable.

The moral of this story is that a model has to go wherever the wind takes him or her—regardless of boyfriends, family, or pets—and cannot have any preconceived notions about his or her appearance or where he or she will be living. And another thing that you should learn from this story is that agencies definitely know a great deal more about the modeling business than you do. I wasted years of potential earning power, at a time when I could have been having a successful career. Models don't have time to waste, especially in the high-fashion world, and most careers last only a few years as age is a *huge* consideration, and opportunities need to be seized immediately when presented.

The older models and commercial print models (both men *and* women) do not have to move around so much. Younger girls (around ages fourteen to twenty-one) and guys (age seventeen and up) cater to the more trendy fashions and have to chase whatever is "en vogue" at the moment, which may involve intense traveling abroad. Those models not going for high fashion may still find that relocating to a larger city can be more lucrative. But no matter who you are or where you live, you have to chase the clients. They will not come and find you!

DO YOUR EXPECTATIONS MATCH YOUR GOALS?

This is where many people can be misled by the hype of the modeling world. I made a simple chart for you, which can act as a guideline for the categories I've taught you about.

TYPE OF WORK	HIGH FASHION	COMM. PRINT	SHOWROOM	FIT	PROMO
A lot of travel	X				
Catalog jobs	X	X			
Advertising jobs	X	X			
Magazine work	X	X			
Music videos	X	X	X		
Standing for hours			X	X	X
Large audiences			X		X
One-on-one selling			X		X
Trade shows			X		X

Do you like to travel? The high-fashion world (as I have said before) is mainly about traveling. You have to follow the trends! If you work in a smaller market (a smaller city that has work for models on a local scale), eventually you will want to work your way up to a larger market (like New York City, where the work for models is expansive, ranging from local work to international catalogs or campaigns), or even go overseas to appear in those coveted European magazines. The usual path for a beginning model from a smaller town in the United States is to go to a secondary market (like Chicago, Seattle, or perhaps Toronto) first, to build the pictures in his or her portfolio. Smaller markets (cities smaller than New York City or Los Angeles) are great for a model to gain experience.

Then from a smaller market he or she may go to Europe to get what are called "tear sheets" or "editorials" from the European market. Tear sheets and editorial work are basically the same thing—magazine fashion stories or covers to put in your portfolio to show your experience as a model. The more you have, the better work you will get *anywhere* in the States, especially in New York. Displaying your work history is kind of like showing a résumé in the corporate world. The way a model builds his or her experience to show in a portfolio is with magazine work, but the best magazines—the more creative and artsy ones, according to the fashion world—are in Europe, and therefore involve all that traveling I keep writing about.

One of the disadvantages of building your portfolio editorially though is that it doesn't pay enough money to cover your expenses, although it *is* necessary, similar to paying your dues by doing an internship at a large corporation. Also the lag time for a magazine to come out on newsstands is sometimes four months or longer. Another downside to focusing on your editorial is when a model first goes abroad—let's say to Paris, for example—he or she may not work in that market, but may be sent to see clients in another editorial market such as Milan. In each market it takes about a minimum of two months to figure out how much you are going to work there . . . so you see how all of a sudden you can be a world traveler in this business *before* you even start making enough of a profit to support yourself. High-fashion agencies often will advance plane fare, hotel, and sometimes spending money for you to start your career in a foreign market or in New York City until you are working enough to pay them back. If a foreign agency doesn't advance anything before you get to their country, they will usually at least advance a photo shoot and some composites, which you can then use to begin seeing clients to get work. I'll go through this in detail in chapter 3, including how to get the most money you can out of an agency before you even start, but remember, the less money you are advanced, the less money you will owe when you start working!

If you really desire to be in the high-fashion world, you will certainly have to eventually move to a bigger fashion-oriented city like New York, London, Paris, or Milan—or perhaps live in all four! There is no way to get around this, because *Vogue* magazine will not come out to the country to book models, and magazines like *Vogue* book models all over the world for their international issues. Magazine editors will sit in their plush offices in the city where they are based, waiting until they find what they are looking for, knowing that potential models will be sent to *them*, not the other way around.

IF YOU DO NOT FIT THE
HIGH-FASHION CATEGORY

Models whose names you will never know, or whose faces you will never recognize, are the skeleton of support holding up the high-fashion industry. It is very similar to when you are watching television and you think to yourself, "I have seen that face before, but I can't remember what show he or she appeared in last." In television there are also the extras, who the audience barely sees, but they are all an integral part of the movie, and the set would not be complete without them. Not everyone on television and in movies is identifiable or has made a name people recognize immediately. Well, it's the same way in modeling—there are girls and guys doing printwork for product advertising (selling cars, household products, etc.), called commercial print or lifestyle models; you probably see their images all the time but do not know their names—they are not well-known supermodels like Heidi Klum. Then there are the "extra" models who are in the backgrounds of those advertisements, and finally, the "behind the scenes" models (similar to technical people working in a movie) doing fit and showroom work who will never even be in front of a camera during their whole modeling career.

The models whose faces are hardly ever shown in public (or in front of the camera) are constantly working behind the scenes in designers' showrooms and manufacturers' offices. These models help put together the clothing that is manufactured around the world. I call them the "behind the camera" support. Designers often need models the same sizes as either the supermodel on the runway or the average-size consumer, because there is a need to fit an outfit on someone in both of those cases before the clothing is shown on the runway, and/or distributed in the stores. Plastic mannequins are helpful for this kind of work, but the clients usually prefer a "live" fit or showroom model so they can see how the fabric moves with the person, and they are able to ask the model questions about how an article of clothing feels. A live person also gives a more genuine feel as to how the fabric is going to drape. Or if an outfit is pulling somewhere that just does not feel right, a person (as opposed to a mannequin) can say something about it.

How do you feel about working at trade shows or conventions? Are you good in one-on-one situations? There is a lot of this type of work in "promotional modeling," which is also called "live" modeling. If you have a flair for selling, and are not shy in public settings, then this is a good area for you. Sometimes promotional modeling involves travel for long-term bookings, but you do not *have* to travel, as is the case with high-fashion modeling. There are specific agencies that specialize in promotional modeling—you already learned about one of them. You can dabble in this type of work to make some extra money while you are trying to get into a print modeling agency; you would be surprised at the amount of work there is. One girl I met got offered a *six-month* spokesmodel contract for a makeup company while working a promotional job! So there absolutely is potential in this type of industry for long-term work, you just have to put yourself out there and see what happens.

Another "live" (not printwork but in front of a live audience) form of modeling is showroom modeling. Promotional modeling is mainly *promoting products* (not fashion); showroom modeling is mainly "promoting" *fashion,* so a lot of showroom models are either in the high-fashion category, or at least have a "look" that resembles a fashion model. Showroom models often work at trade shows as well, but this category presents fewer one-on-one situations, such as in promotional modeling, and the difference is mainly the type of audience, and the kind of company that is trying to market their product. Showroom work can be a miniversion of runway modeling; some designers even have shows, often called "presentations," that mimic the ones during Fashion Week in New York City. And other showroom modeling consists of smaller "minishows" right there in the designer's showroom or office area at different times during the year. Designers often need showroom models to "show" the clothing for their clients who buy selected pieces to put in department stores, or for their press clients, who write reviews.

Are you in your early to mid twenties? If you are, what do you think of commercial print modeling? There *are* other divisions in high-fashion agencies for older and more sophisticated models, but you should definitely consider commercial print modeling as well, because you do not want to limit your potential income. Even if you *do* get signed with a more fashion-oriented sophisticated division or even the main division in a high-fashion agency, you can *still* have a separate commercial print agency. Commercial print agencies are usually non-exclusive, and you can work with both agencies without a conflict, which means your fashion modeling agency will not be getting calls for commercial print, and your commercial print agency will not be getting the same calls as the fashion agency. Commercial print is also so wide open these days to every type of look, so it is worth it to send your pictures in just to see what happens.

I spoke to Stacy Rosen at the Greer Lange Model and Talent Agency in Philadelphia who specializes in commercial print modeling, and asked her about the commercial print world. My first question was whether breaking into commercial print modeling entailed the same process as trying to break into high-fashion modeling. And her answer was that it is almost the same. "Unfortunately, the whole modeling industry has some sort of stigma that you need professional pictures before you join an agency. But that just isn't the case. We do prefer that you send a few digital pictures for consideration, and we can recommend good commercial photographers and the types of photos you'll need if we choose to work with you. This helps you to avoid the common mistake of spending money on the wrong pictures, or poorly taken pictures."

I also wondered if the commercial print world looks for more of a mainstream type of model, including age ranges, and she replied that "a lot of the work we book is for models between the ages of thirty and forty-five! Commercial print involves more 'real life' types of models, and where high fashion may have the need for younger or more unique looks from their models, commercial print clients are actually looking for a simpler type of model who can make their products appealing on the mass market being sold to many different audiences at once."

Another question I asked was one that I thought you should hear the answer to from an industry expert other than me. What should someone expect after getting representation with a modeling agency? "Any model that joins any agency should realize that just because you don't need pictures before you join an agency, it doesn't mean that you aren't going to have to get professional photos and spend money to market yourself *after* you start your modeling career. Every type of model, from high fashion to commercial print, needs to have professional-looking photos and marketing materials after they are with an agency, which means paying for pictures from time to time, including updating your portfolio with new photo shoots when necessary. This is a business, and it involves investing in yourself to start working, as well as staying in the business for as long as you can."

Well, what kind of money should a model prepare to invest initially? Stacy's view (and most people in the modeling industry will agree) is that "it really depends on the person, and how well they take pictures on the first few photo shoots. Pictures for your portfolio can be from $300 and up, and it may take two to three photo shoots to get a working portfolio together in the beginning. It all depends on your abilities in front of the camera, and how much money you have to spend on your career before you start working. But if you don't have representation at an agency, there is no reason for professional pictures, unless you are working with a manager for development." And that fact right there, ladies and gentlemen, should be adhered to at all times, no matter *what* kind of model you are trying to eventually become.

Stacy also mentioned that "industrial" work is quite common for a model who is working in commercial print. Industrial work is similar to commercial work on television. It makes use of acting skills and involves creating corporate training videos, taping demonstrations within a corporation, and other nonpublic uses. Industrial work may not be as glamorous as commercial work on television, but can be just as lucrative and provides more opportunities for work, especially in the regional markets. Industrial work also helps you hone your skills and groom yourself for potential commercial work, which I'll tell you more about in chapter 5. Philadelphia has a lot of this type of work, as well as other smaller regional markets in the United States like Detroit, Chicago, Washington, D.C., and Greensboro, North Carolina, to name a few. I was quite surprised when I spoke to the owner of Directions USA, an agency in Greensboro, about the endless types of industrials that they book.

Commercial print modeling, showroom, and fit modeling can also be a lucrative way to be in the business. The rates aren't as high but still pay an average of $75 to $300 or more an hour. Also, there is generally more consistent work, especially in the showroom and fit categories. Clients who book fit models do not care as much about the age of a girl (as opposed to high fashion), as they do about her being the exact measurements that they need for their sample clothing, so that specialty has more longevity than print work. When I worked at Ford Models in New York, their fit division models were at one point making more money than *any* of the other divisions! And commercial print in general (like high-fashion print) contains a good bit of advertising, so there is excellent potential income there as well.

Note about advertising: it pays more than catalog work, because it involves more exposure of the model. The more a model is seen in public (for example, in magazines, on billboards, kiosks, sides of buses, etc.) the more he or she gets paid to do the job. There are exceptions, of course, like when a model does a high-profile campaign that forwards *her* career more than it does the designer because the designer is already well known, but that is more often seen in the high-fashion area, and there are countless exceptions in that category.

MAKING SENSE OF IT ALL

The reason I have tried to give you an idea of what is involved in each area of modeling, and provided the categories chart, is to help you try and find out on a realistic level what kind of model you would like to be. This prepares you for chapter 3, which deals with promotion, where you will learn about target marketing yourself for a more efficient marketing process, just as the managers and scouts do. You don't want to be promoting yourself in markets where your look doesn't fit, but on the other hand, you want to make sure you hit all the markets that you can that are appropriate for you and are, at the same time, tailored to your personal type of look. These questions will also help you "realize" yourself as a model.

Sometimes answering these questions can help you devise realistic goals as you start a career in the fashion industry. For example, let's review the question that asks how you see yourself as a model. If you imagine yourself modeling in a couture fashion show but don't fit the high-fashion category specifications, then you need to revert back to the category descriptions and choose a different category, or start working on the things that you can do to be in that chosen category, if that is a realistic option for you.

Now, select one or two of the categories from the list that you just learned about that you feel characterize you best—make sure you meet *each* requirement for that category, whether there are only a couple of requirements or a half dozen. Take your physical measurements and compare them to the category that you believe fits you most appropriately. Though you may select more than one category, you *must* be specific about meeting the requirements. If you start marketing yourself in the wrong category (one that doesn't fit you), your chances will plummet instantly. I will explain the reason for this in chapter 3, about promotion, but don't jump ahead! You'll learn it when you need to.

When you are finished selecting a category, combine it with your psychological perspective (the questions you asked yourself) and double-check the chart I made for you. Write down these choices so you have something positive to work toward. Put those categories (or category) in bright capital letters, hang it up someplace where you will see it every day, and believe that you can make it happen with hard work and determination. If you have to change these choices later, after you have exhausted your resources or your measurements have changed, you should allow yourself to do so with the attitude of moving forward and finding your niche—not the mind-set of failure. It is too early on to discuss negative feedback from agencies because maintaining a healthy outlook and a positive attitude is half the battle in modeling, as well as in everyday living! Don't worry, after you have finished this book, you will know what other choices you have if your first category selection does not work out. My mother used to say that anything worth having takes hard work . . . and that is how you should look at this business. Make sure you are mentally and physically ready for this business, because it is one roller coaster of a ride!

Fitness

The most difficult part of the preparation process (for most of you) is staying fit. As hard as it is, it is imperative that you get and stay fit. *Every* category of models *has* to be fit; there are no exceptions. Even plus models have to be in shape . . . I'm not talking about getting ready for the Olympics, but you have to be in decent shape where you are confident of your body image, and physically toned and ready to present yourself in front of people. One of the myths of modeling regarding fitness is that people think "my face is enough to get me signed with an agency"—not true, ladies and gentlemen! The *Webster's Dictionary* definition of "model" is: "a standard or example for imitation or comparison"—which means that *you,* as a model, set the trend, and you are being watched and critiqued every second; and it's not just your face. You are aiming to break into a business where corporate America will be trying to sell their products through you, and most often you will be holding or standing next to the product (or wearing it, as in the case of designer clothing), and your look coming from within is a big part of the image that a particular company or designer pays you to pull off, but your body comes in a close second. Also, your face may take on a different shape, depending on your weight—for example, your face may be more angular if you are at a lower weight than usual—so body and face are all intertwined.

Proportion plays a great role in your physical appearance; you should not be oversized or undersized in any one place on your body. That includes men as well! Being *too* buff is not a plus in the modeling world, but being in shape with toned muscles is. As a woman can have too large a hip size, a man can have shoulders that are too big from lifting weights, or thighs that will not fit into average-size pants that are used for photo shoots or on the runway. The way to keep track of this is to go by my measurements and sizes under the category descriptions. If you meet the measurement guidelines but not the dress or suit size, or vice versa, then something is wrong and you have to fix it with exercise and/or your diet. Remember ladies, lifting weights sometimes makes a person *bigger* than they normally would be! Lighter weights with more repetition may be something you want to consider if you are too bulky in the muscle department and are considering a career in modeling.

If you can't afford it, you do not have to go out and join a gym, because right in your own house there are simple exercises you can do to start getting yourself into shape. For light cardio, a twenty-five-minute brisk walk around your neighborhood every day will make a big difference within weeks. Inside your house you can work on defining your body with lunges, sit-ups, push-ups, butt tucks, and leg lifts for thirty minutes every other day, and it will start producing results in just a few weeks. This is a business!!! Work hard at it. Stretch those muscles before and after exercise to keep them toned. Both men and women should be careful not to bulk up *too* much. If you are interested in taking classes, yoga and Pilates classes are everywhere, and always have beginning instruction.

If you can afford a gym, go join one now! It will benefit you in the long run not only personally but also professionally, in modeling. There are student discounts at some of the gyms, for those of you in school. People who work out regularly have more energy, look and *feel* better, and usually maintain a healthier lifestyle in general. Eating right and working out go hand in hand—the perfect combination for looking good on the outside *and* feeling good on the inside.

A word about dieting: Anyone who feels they need to diet should contact a registered dietician or doctor on how to do it in a *healthy* way. I do not in any way promote men or women eating less unless they are well informed on how to do so the *right* way. Two models have died in the past few years from eating disorders (not including models we may not have heard about), and there are always models who have to postpone their career because they get *too* skinny—I have seen it happen many times! The entire fashion industry has been emphasizing good health as it moves forward into the twenty-first century, which is what you should also do. Yes, certain types of models need to be slimmer than others, but there is a way to lose weight and get in shape that will benefit your modeling career in addition to your overall future health. And take your time—crash dieting is *so* bad for you! Plus, there is more of a chance you will instantly gain back the weight you lost if you crash diet. Don't worry, the agencies will still be around by the time you are ready! If not, then be glad that you waited and did not sign with an agency that is not around anymore. Seriously, though, it will only benefit you to take pictures or go to see people with the best body that you can have—and that means looking and staying healthy.

As long as you have followed everything I said precisely so far, you are ready to go and take the pictures that you will be sending to the agencies. Chapter 2 will show you how to do that, and what rules to live by for the promotion process, which is described in chapter 3. Remember, you *have* to be in shape. This is *not negotiable*.

Making a Commitment

By now you have learned about the way agencies are set up, the different types of modeling, how to figure out where you fit in as a model, and some of the basics of fitness and nutrition. Before we go on, you should make a commitment to yourself that you are going to try everything in this book that I tell you to, no matter how silly or trivial it may seem.

I created a process based on twenty years of experience in the modeling world, a method that I know both works and is *the* method preferred by modeling agencies. The *only way* it will benefit you to the maximum is to follow my advice precisely. The way the inner workings of the modeling world are and the way this world is perceived are two very different views. You need to trust that I know what I am talking about and make your commitment to this process that I am teaching you.

The reason this commitment is so important is because you are not entering an easy business. It is a world full of personal rejections, conflicting advice, and highly charged attitudes and opinions. And like any business, modeling has both its ups and downs. It's a business where you have to stay on top of everything—your weight, the way you dress, your skin, teeth, hair, maintaining a positive attitude, and on and on. You need to keep plugging away *no matter what*. Please do not give up unless you really feel that you have exhausted all of your resources and are simply not getting anywhere. The resources I'm discussing here do not include money, of course—I repeat myself over and over again about not spending your money to break into this business because I want to make sure this point hits home. Spending unnecessary funds will not get you instant representation—there is *no such thing with a legitimate modeling agency.*

If you do not get the response from agencies that you want at first, take a step back, give yourself some time off, and remarket yourself differently, which I will explain how to do in chapter 5. If you follow what is in this book and still do not get any response, then a career in modeling may not be for you. And please understand that there is *no such thing* as buying your way to become a model. Unfortunately there are no guarantees in the modeling business, but I am definitely giving you the best chance you have with my four-step process.

Before You Take Your Pictures

Now that you fully understand how important it is to be completely committed to the steps I outline in this book, go back and look at your choices, and make sure you are totally ready to start taking your pictures for your marketing campaign. Be precise about your measurements, make sure you are completely aware of what each category entails, and be confident about your own unique look to get ready and sell yourself to other people.

You are going to be selling yourself as a product, and that takes a bit of subjectivity while also constantly reevaluating yourself. Confidence in who you are makes it easier to assess yourself in the end, because you can be more critical of what you are as a commodity, in a positive way, of course. Being impartial about your looks is not an easy task!

So take a deep breath, know that you are the best that you can be, and take some amazing pictures! I've made the process as simple as possible, to bring out the *real* you, and to show modeling agencies the kind of pictures that they are looking for, whether they receive them by the mail or by e-mail during your promotion step. Simplicity is the key when taking these pictures, so please don't be distracted by the creations of fashion magazines and catalogs or advertising images. Just do precisely what I say, and you will get the most accurate response possible—I promise!

PICTURES

Pictures are your main marketing tool and will be used to promote you throughout a career in modeling. One of the biggest myths in the modeling industry is that you need professional pictures to get noticed by modeling agencies. This is *simply not true*. Nonprofessional pictures are actually *preferred* by modeling agencies, and in this chapter I will teach you how to take them.

This picture-taking process really works—it's what I did in my position as a scout every day!!! I have placed models with European agencies with just Polaroid pictures when I was a new scout, even though the agencies had no idea who I was, . . . and they advanced plane fare, hotel, pictures, and composites! I most recently placed a young girl who got several requests from high-fashion agencies in New York City, using pictures her *brother* took—and after visiting several agencies in person, she ended up choosing New York Models as her final pick. The pictures that got her so much attention were taken in her backyard in Ohio! She just followed my directions for what agencies were looking for, and they turned out beautifully. So as I said, simplicity is best. All you need is a digital, disposable, or Polaroid camera. Either way, whichever camera you use, what matters in the end is *how and what kind of pictures you take.*

Why You Shouldn't Pay for Pictures Without an Agency

More than likely, any professional pictures you take on your own will be thrown out by your agency when you agree to work with them as a model in any category. Why does this happen? Well, I'll explain why by breaking down the process of how new models get started once they are with a modeling agency.

"Test" is a word you should know before getting into the modeling industry. *Every* model at *every* level will "test" for new photos to improve a portfolio, but especially brand-new models. A "test" is simply a photo shoot where the model poses for pictures for his or her book. Sometimes a test photo shoot is for both the model *and* the photographer, so the photographer can use the pictures in his or her portfolio as well. (If this is the case, the test pictures should be at no cost to you, or you should only be paying for expenses to the photographer, such as film and processing). The same goes for any stylists or hair and makeup artists who are involved in the shoot as well. If they are using the pictures for their portfolio too, they should not be charging you for their services.

The people working in an agency interview photographers to take pictures for their models at discounted rates, or for free. They are called "test photographers." These photographers specialize in taking photos of new models, or for a particular agency. Any photographer that you find on your own will more than likely not be a photographer that a modeling agency would select as a test photographer. You see, modeling agencies are very specific in their choices for test photographers (especially in the larger markets), and a new model's eye is not trained to rate a photographer's approach to lighting, styling, makeup, and art direction. The agency also likes to have a close relationship with the test photographers, so that they can have a hand in deciding what the pictures will look like with the photographer before the photo shoot. If you *do* find a photographer who claims to have an affiliation with a modeling agency, please ask him or her for a referral, and call the agency to double-check. Don't take anyone's word without checking references! This is the beginning of creating your own, unique, individual look plus an image to go with that look, and your modeling agent or manager should have a say every step of the way in marketing your image. This is impossible if you try to do the pictures in your portfolio by yourself.

High-fashion modeling agencies that take on brand-new models, especially when the models are younger (approximately the teenage years), usually have what is called a "new faces" or "development" board. This division focuses on molding a new model's career and is found only in high-fashion divisions. The agents in a new-faces division will be a little more meticulous about testing and creating a model's image, because this is the point where potential supermodels start their careers. The models in this division will test many times over, as they are being groomed for high-end work.

In every other category other than high fashion, there is still a certain type of look to go with that category, and the agents know best what sells in a particular market. There is not a separate testing division for older models or commercial print, but the agents will still take the time to mold you accordingly to a particular market's demands in that geographical area, and to what image the agency as a whole is trying to achieve. If the agency is huge and has thousands of models, sometimes there isn't a strong definition of what image that agency is trying to get across, but they still will have their own select photographers to photograph you in the most appropriate way for your portfolio.

Sometimes a test shoot will produce only one or two usable pictures, other times more than that. Test photo shoots are also good practice, because after the film gets developed, you can examine the contact sheets, which show every photo of the shoot, to see which ways you move that make you look best, or which facial expressions work for you and which ones do not. Every model needs to constantly test, not just for practice or to get better pictures in his or her portfolio—although those are good reasons by themselves—but because the looks of fashion are constantly changing, and clients can instantly tell whether you are using recent or outdated pictures. If you get a chance to test with a photographer for free, you probably should. But, once again, do not spend any money taking pictures *before* signing with a modeling agency, because there is not much of a chance you are going to use those pictures, and if you do, it won't be long before you get better ones that you and your agency decide on together. Creating a portfolio takes the expertise of a manager or modeling agent, and that is one of the biggest reasons why you should not undertake this task on your own.

Nonprofessional pictures of you *really are* the best way to enter into the modeling industry! The agencies usually tell people to just bring casual family photos when going on an open call or to send in pictures, because they can't take the time to tell people what they *really* want—the kind of specific photos that I'm going to teach you how to take based on my experience as a manager, agent, and scout. Anyone can tell you to "send in pictures" to a modeling agency, but what *kind* of pictures, how many, and how to take them is crucial to your overall marketing strategy. People working at modeling agencies are experts at creating the image that they need in order to sell you, so put your trust in them *after* you get representation and for now, put your trust in me for getting them to notice *you*.

Nathalie Bernier, a former director of Elite Model Management in New York City for several years, and also previously a director at Next Model Management in New York City, agrees that it is important *not* to pay for your pictures while trying to gain representation as a model. Ms. Bernier stresses the all-important rule to remember, which is that "breaking into the modeling industry should *not cost you a thing!!* You don't need to go to a photographer who will charge you a fortune to take your first pictures or any other pictures before joining an agency, but have them done by a friend or member of the family with a digital or disposable camera."

Just how critical is it to take the right types of pictures to send to agencies? Ms. Bernier responded that it is really crucial to send the correct nonprofessional pictures, even if it seems like such a simple and basic thing to do. Quite often pictures of new faces at modeling agencies are overlooked just because they are not appropriate. You need to send different types of pictures in the ways which are going to allow agencies to see you in the best possible manner, with all the requirements necessary (for example, beautiful features, height, weight, posture, etc.).

I also asked Ms. Bernier which picture, of the seven pictures I teach people to take, does she think is the most important? "In my opinion, the head shot facing the camera is the most important one, since whoever looks at your pictures will probably use this photo to determine if he or she is going to continue to look at the other pictures or not. But make sure *all* the pictures are clear, in focus, and your very best work."

Finally, one of the most important tips about appearance for women is not to pile on the makeup—here is what Ms. Bernier says about makeup in the pictures that are sent to agencies: "It is highly important that a model (especially in high fashion) take her first pictures *without* make up, except for maybe a touch of lip gloss. This way, modeling agencies have an accurate way of seeing what he or she really looks like. Quite often young girls feel that they need to use makeup to look better, but the truth is that agents and scouts are looking for more genuine beauties, and it is a necessity for them to detect beautiful skin or features naturally from your photos, and makeup tends to hide a person's true beauty, or at least, the kind of beauty that modeling agents are always searching for. Older models can get away with wearing makeup, but it needs to be applied carefully, so one can barely notice it."

The Importance of Not Wearing Makeup

As Ms. Bernier said, modeling agencies like to see new faces in their raw form, and so do the clients when you're a working model! When you become a model, the only makeup you should be wearing is on a photo shoot, where the makeup artist creates your look, or if you have a pimple on your face or something else small enough to cover. If you put makeup on, it changes your look and doesn't leave room for anyone

to imagine what your potential is as a model. For example, as a modeling agent, when I look at a model's face I try to imagine what different
looks a girl or a guy has the potential to achieve, and as a casting director, I need to envision a model on my photo shoot. Without makeup, it
is a lot easier for me to do just that.

Modeling *used* to be about dark makeup like Twiggy once wore, and
overdone hair, such as Farrah Fawcett's feathered hairdo, but as we become more of a fuss-free nation in the twenty-first century, wearing jeans
more than ever and realizing that "natural is sexy," the image of modeling
is changing. And the rest of the world is following too. Use makeup *only*
for covering blemishes and circles under your eyes—if you have more
makeup on than that, you may look as if you are simply trying too hard,
and that is the complete opposite of what I want agents to think of you.

Models are not perfect in person, as a matter of fact, quite the opposite. They are people too! Don't let airbrushing, retouching, and makeup
fool you. If you are thinking that you want to look like one of the models in the magazines, who has a made-up face and immaculately styled
hair, please *put that idea to rest right now*. First of all, the pictures are retouched and airbrushed in magazines and catalogs. Secondly, the way
those girls or guys *made it* to that high of a level in modeling was by *not*
wearing a lot of makeup to their castings and appointments! When those
models met with the clients to book the jobs, I guarantee you they went
with freshly scrubbed faces without makeup.

By the way, agents can spot a great potential look no matter if you
have a few pimples or if your hair isn't perfect. Whether you are going
to be sending pictures to agents or seeing them in person, the more
casual and natural you are, the better it is to see the real you. This
school of thought goes for both the younger *and* the older people in the
crowd. It is always better to wait until you look your best, but if something like pimples are an ongoing problem for you, try selling yourself
on the days when your skin looks its best. Please—let the photos do the
talking, not your fire engine red lipstick and bleach blond hair streaks.

You may think that wearing makeup is not such a big deal, but that
is why I am writing this book, because people do not fully understand
what the modeling industry is looking for. People try to translate what
they *think* modeling agencies want. Since this is a business that is too

complicated to figure out on your own, let me point you in the right direction and give you the proper tools you need.

Take the Perfect Pictures

Are you ready to start taking your pictures? Modeling agencies need to remember who you are, whether it be when you walk out the door of an open call, or if you are sending pictures in the mail. Please follow these instructions carefully. Though they may seem tedious at times, every detail is necessary in creating the final product. And the more you practice, the easier the process will be.

There are three things to consider in taking good pictures:

1. Your *appearance*
2. The *types* of pictures to take
3. *How to shoot* these types of pictures to make you look your best

APPEARANCE

Your appearance is of course what is going to be the decision-making factor in your quest for breaking into the modeling industry. You must not "try" to be what you think a model represents; you have to be yourself. As models have different personalities, so do modeling agencies. Let them mold to you. It's kind of like being in a relationship. You want you and your partner to fit together without too much effort. It's a serious commitment, but it's still meant to be fun, right? Well, so is the modeling industry! As much as I try to tell you to approach this like any other business, it's still a fun and exciting industry. But if you go around trying to adapt to what you think each agency is looking for, then in the meantime you are going to lose the real "you," which is your primary selling point. If you just try to be yourself, in the midst of all the rules and technical advice I give you, then the rest will follow. I realize sometimes it's hard when you're concentrating on posing and lighting and everything else, but that is why I encourage you to practice. It gets much easier over time, and like riding a bike or driving, you soon do not have to think about the steps in between, just the whole picture of going somewhere.

Follow these next rules precisely when you are about to take your pictures. *Do not break even one rule.* Trust me, I am here to help you, and these are the cardinal rules in creating your image as a "new face."

1. **NO MAKEUP FOR HIGH-FASHION HOPEFULS OR CHILDREN; *VERY* LIGHT MAKEUP FOR OTHER CATEGORIES, EXCEPT FOR MEN.** I have already stressed the importance of this issue, so let me describe the execution. The "very light makeup" for women should *only* be for covering facial blemishes or dark circles under the eyes with a cover stick, putting a sheer gloss on the lips, light mascara, or some sheer powder for shine. Keep it fresh, clean, and natural-looking. Make sure that no one can see foundation lines on your neck, or powder marks in the creases of your eyes. Any makeup other than the things I listed is a big turnoff to anyone in the modeling industry. If you are older, it doesn't matter, that is *you*, and you can't change it with makeup. Fifty is the new forty, and forty is the new thirty . . . the public opinion of older people in advertising is changing all the time toward the positive—so if you are an "older" model trying to get into the business, do it with pride and confidence that you look incredible for your age.

   If you are a man, do not even wear powder. Don't worry about covering up things on your face. Male modeling is very different from female modeling, and agents do not expect any makeup, although male models *do* wear makeup on photo shoots (mostly powder), but that is a different story. Once you start working, you will get "groomed" on the set of a professional photo shoot. There are even people called "groomers" who specialize in hair and makeup for male models! Male model bookers are well trained to spot men without all the fuss from makeup or hairstyling.

2. **FINGERNAILS SHOULD HAVE NO POLISH, OR CLEAR POLISH.** Beige is okay, as long as it is sheer. Have your nails

trimmed short, as agents do not want to see long nails. Neutral color polish is perfect, because it gives a smooth look to your hands, instead of a bright color chopping up the elegant lines on a hand.

3. **DO NOT WEAR ANY HATS, SCARVES, OR BANDANAS.** If you do, it will look like you are trying to cover something, and an agent looking at a picture of someone wearing head gear will just wish they could see what was underneath. If an agent only has pictures to go by and can't ask you to take off your hat, or whatever it is that you're wearing, your chances of getting a favorable response diminish. It will be assumed that you are trying to cover something up, and your pictures will go in the trash. The agent will move on to the next set of pictures, where the person can be seen clearly. I don't mean to sound harsh, but that is exactly what happens, and I promised myself when I wrote this book I would be as honest as I could with you, my reader.

4. **HAIR SHOULD BE CLEAN AND NATURAL-LOOKING, WELL TRIMMED, NO RADICAL COLORS OR STREAKS, NO HAIRSPRAY OR FANCY UPDOS.** You want to keep your hair as simple as possible, especially in the pictures where it is not up in a headband or an elastic. Hair can really be a distraction from your face, and you do not want that distraction working against you. If you think your hair is your best feature, great! It will show in the pictures I'll teach you to take where your hair is down. Even if your hair is your best feature, your face is still the part of you with the most expression, and it should not be hiding behind your hair.

5. **NO JEWELRY OR PIERCINGS ON YOUR BODY THAT ANYONE CAN SEE.** Jewelry is a *huge* distraction!! You want a potential agent or manager looking at *you*—not trying to guess what kind of gemstone your belly ring is made with.

6. **FOR THE HEAD SHOTS, PROFILE, AND THREE-QUARTER SHOT, MEN AND WOMEN SHOULD WEAR A VERY PLAIN OUTFIT.** I know it sounds crazy, but anything else will detract attention from your face. A fitted T-shirt or tank top is

great, no patterns or bold colors, with nicely fitted jeans on the bottom. Wearing a fancy dress or a suit will make it look as if you are trying too hard. Look casual—but still wear something that is formfitting, so anyone looking at the picture can tell what your body frame looks like. Also think about the background you are shooting against. For example, a white T-shirt would not work if you are shooting the pictures against a white wall. It will make you blend into the wall too much, and an agent wouldn't be able to see where your body begins and ends.

7. MEN MUST WEAR SWIM TRUNKS AND WOMEN MUST WEAR A TWO-PIECE BATHING SUIT FOR THE BODY SHOTS. Men, I repeat, *swim trunks,* not Speedos or thongs! Boxers are appropriate if you do not have a conservative swimsuit. And women, please do not wear thongs either. Save your thongs and Speedos for South Beach; agents do not want to see them *ever.* If you have an amazing body, you can show it off with swim trunks for a guy or a Brazilian-cut bathing suit for the women. Plus, a thong will distract the viewer from what you are trying to achieve—having them look at *you* and not your skimpy swimsuit. Also, wear a suit that does not have eye-catching patterns or neon colors. A simple bathing suit shape in a solid color is the best way for showing off the most important thing—*you.*

8. YOU SHOULD BE BAREFOOTED. This goes for both men and women. Yes, heels look nice on women wearing a swimsuit, but it is not appropriate for sending in pictures for the first time. Simplicity is the best approach for the types of pictures you are going to take.

FOR THE MEN ONLY

Men have a variety of "looks," just like the female models. If you are younger than twenty-five or so years old, you have the option of having long hair, wearing casual dress, or creating a waiflike physical appearance. An older male model usually can't get away with these attributes, because product marketing toward older men usually involves a model having a more clean-cut appearance. But the one serious advantage that men have is that it is okay to be older! The fashion world for women almost obsessively focuses on younger female models, but the men have more of a chance of working at an older age, if you have the right look. There *is* a little less work for male models as opposed to female models, but there is also less competition.

To shave or not to shave. . . . I'm not a man—if you haven't noticed already—but I was a male model agent at a reputable men's agency for a while, and also as a casting director I booked male models for catalogs, magazines, and advertising. The main issue regarding male models shaving or not shaving is that they usually look drastically different each way, and clients looking for male models have a preset image in their heads of what they want—either "clean-cut" or "unshaven." Like I have said before, guys who do not shave are usually younger hipsters who are going after the supermodel status, and their look is very specific. And even then, there are not a lot of goatees, just a couple of days of growth on the face. That is not to say that guys who shave have no chance at the brass ring; they absolutely do. I'm just trying to tell you the difference so you will pick one look and stick with it, as I stressed in chapter 1, under "Model Identification."

So, should you shave? It is preferable, but that is up to you. You have to try to figure out how you best see yourself. Shaven is more often than not the best way to present yourself for a first impression. It leaves you open to show off your jawbone structure, which is very important in male modeling. If you still do not know which way to go with the shaving, I suggest that you market yourself shaven first and see what the response is. It shows off your skin and jawbone, which may otherwise be covered if you do not shave. A prominent jawbone is a big bonus in the male modeling industry, so show it off if you think yours is amazing!

Specific Types of Pictures to Take

Now that you have learned the basics for getting yourself ready to take pictures, I will show you the types of photographs you need to have, whether you are mailing pictures in or going to visit agencies in person. The good news is that you can use the same type of pictures for both of these purposes. You will need to leave these pictures with the agency or manager when on an open call so they remember you, in addition to the pictures you send out with your mailings and e-mails.

If you are marketing yourself via mailings and/or e-mail, as op-posed to attending open calls, then the kinds of pictures you take are especially important. You must give the best first impression you can when someone is not seeing you in person for the first time. This in-cludes taking color pictures that are clear, in focus, have natural light-ing, and pictures that show the real you without makeup or distracting clothing or jewelry.

Open calls are beneficial because you can see modeling agencies in person, but they limit you to one geographical area. What if you are not living in the ideal area for maximizing your potential? And even if you are, you should expand your horizons to see what other markets might think about your look. That is the purpose of putting together these pictures of yourself and then sending them out—you never know if someone in another market will want you badly enough and what they will offer to get you there.

When you send pictures to agencies by postal mail, they should be limited to the seven scenarios I am going to describe below. All model-ing agents are looking for a specific thing, and to already have your photos in the preferred format will only save time, money, and exas-peration on both sides. It may even open doors for you as well as earn you some respect if you follow exactly what I say; you will look more like a "manager" and will stand out professionally. You will also know that you have done everything you can to market yourself to a partic-ular agency and can then move on to the next step.

An agent's and a manager's eyes are well trained in what to look for in a picture of a new face, so if you follow the correct format, it will be much easier to get discovered. Think about it . . . you walk into a cloth-ing store to buy a nice shirt for a party you have to go to that night, but you only have ten minutes to shop. Isn't it much easier to scan the whole store for what you are looking for if the shirts are nicely hung and in order of color and size, than if all the clothing was thrown in a pile on the floor? Well, that's why I am teaching you the most efficient way to shoot and organize your pictures, and what the agents are looking for, so their eyes do not scan over the picture without seeing it, and you catch their attention with your marketing capabilities. It's all in the presentation! Agents are businesspeople too, they just happen to have the creative job description of looking at pictures of people for a living.

Please read the rest of this chapter *before* taking the following pictures, because I will give you tips on how to stand and pose naturally, and on lighting and background effects in the next section after this one.

1. Take two head shots facing front, from the upper chest up, with your face straight to the camera. Keep your hair down for both of these shots. Take one shot not smiling, and one smiling.

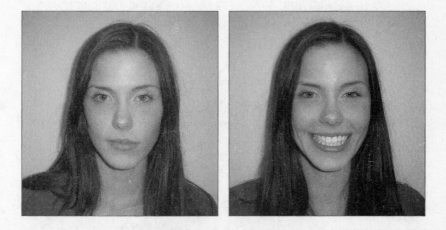

2. Take another head shot facing front, from the upper chest up, with your face straight to the camera, and put your hair up for this picture. Do not smile. This is basically the same picture as in step number one, but with your hair off of your face it shows more of your facial features, like your ears and jawbone, as well as your neck. Women, if your hair is short, either put a clip or headband in the front to keep it away from your face, or if you are a man and your hair is short, slick it back with water or hair gel.

3. You will need one profile shot of your face, from your upper chest up, with your hair off of the face so the agency can see the side angles of your neck and jawbone.

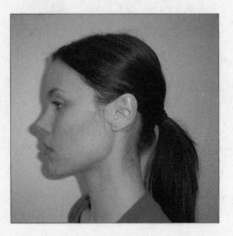

4. For the three-quarter shot, tell whoever is taking the picture to pull back so that he or she can take a picture from your lower hip area to the top of your head. You can throw a little shoulder into this one if you are a female; males, maybe put

your thumb in your front jean pocket. Not too posey, but for this picture you want to have a nice *subtle* shape to your upper body. You will need only one of these, not smiling for the high-fashion hopefuls, and smiles for all the rest of you.

5. Finally, you will need two full-length pictures in a swimsuit (including your bare feet), one facing front looking at the camera, and one from the back with the back of your head toward the camera.

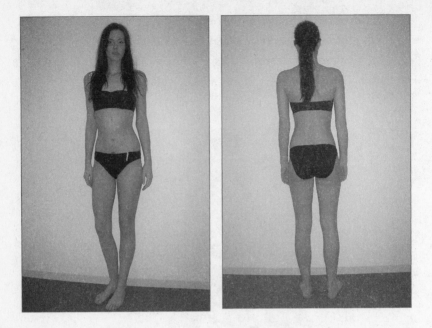

How to Take These Pictures

You do not need to be a professional photographer to get the proper lighting and angles for simple pictures such as these. Remember, these pictures actually should *not* be professional pictures! Have a friend or a family member take them with a digital, disposable, or Polaroid camera. Digital cameras are the best for practicing, then you can take as many as you want, and erase any not-so-perfect pictures. I'm trying to save you a lot of money and show you what agents are really looking for, and it's all in the pictures I am about to show you how to take.

If you go on an open call with a modeling agency, they will most likely take Polaroids or digital pictures of you, so what I'm going to teach you next is also good practice for when you reach that moment. You will know more about the angles at which you shoot best, your face *and* your body, and it will make you more confident when someone shoves a camera in your face all of a sudden at an open call.

Part of going on open calls is dealing with that moment, and modeling agents will watch every move that you make, and how you react to their taking pictures of you in a foreign setting.

TAKE NOTICE OF THE LIGHTING

If you are taking pictures outside, early-morning or late-afternoon sun is best. But if you cannot go outside, try evenly spaced lighting inside. In other words, do not have only one bright lamp in the corner of a dark room. The lighting should be the same all around you in the room, whether you are standing in the corner, or in the middle of that room. One lamp in the corner of the room probably means that as you walk away from it, the light in the room (and on your face) will get darker, and that will not create consistent lighting in your pictures. Uneven lighting often casts shadows, and it is harder to see what you look like with shadows on your face.

On the other hand, if you are outdoors, be careful of the glare of sunlight directly on your face. Too much sunlight, as well as too much lighting in a room, can wash out your features. Make sure you can see each facial feature *clearly;* if they are "washed out" it means your features are not distinctive, and your skin is also probably much lighter in the picture than it is in person.

The pictures also must be taken against a neutral background color (white is preferred). But do not wear white, especially if your background is white—you will blend into the wall. If you are outside and do not have access to a white wall, anything behind you that is not too distracting will do. Just always remember to keep everything around you neutral so it doesn't distract from your beautiful facial features or body.

About skin tones . . . if you have really pale skin, you need to be extra careful about the lighting you are using, and the color of the background that is behind you. If you stand in front of a white background and it tends to wash you out, then play with different colors and find the right choice to show yourself off best. For instance, if you normally have a lot of freckles on your face, and you can't see them in the pictures that were taken, you need to try again. Be realistic though—if you only have a few freckles and they are very light, they will probably not show up on Polaroid film no matter what you do. Try to compare your skin in the pictures with your real skin color—the color should be close in comparison.

CAMERA ANGLES

Shooting pictures at the proper angles is crucial to getting the exact pictures you need to market yourself. Holding the camera the right way takes practice. You will be presenting these pictures to people who look at pictures for a living! If the person who takes your pictures is not paying attention to the way he or she is holding the camera, it will show in the end result. Tilting the camera toward you or away from you even just an inch in the wrong direction can totally alter a face, or make someone appear fatter or skinnier than they really are. Let me give you some friendly tips on how to shoot these pictures.

1. **SHOOTING PICTURES FROM AN ANGLE LOWER THAN YOU IS THE LEAST FLATTERING IN A HEAD SHOT.** Here is an example of too low an angle.

This can cause the chin and neck to look too big and even look as if there is no distinction between the two. And if you're a potential model, you might be taller than the person taking your pictures, so he or she might be standing at an angle naturally lower than you to begin with. If the person who is taking the pictures is shorter than you, tell him or her to stand on a telephone book or stool to be at eye level with you.

2. **SHOOTING PICTURES FROM UP ABOVE CAN CHANGE THE SHAPE OF YOUR FACE.** It is hard to decipher bone structure in someone's face when the camera is shooting from above the subject. Also, the forehead may look bigger than it really is, and that is a big disadvantage to a potential model.

When taking a body shot, exaggerated angles (with the camera held too high or low) do not flatter the body either. For example, look what happens when a body shot is taken from too high an angle.

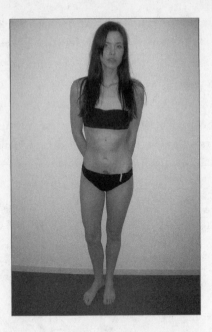

The body can appear a lot shorter than it really is. And from too low, the camera can make you appear several inches taller than you really are.

Although it may seem that being taller is a good thing, you don't want an agency or manager to have an incorrect impression of you. Also, in these last two photos, the model's hands are behind her back and it makes her appear less relaxed than if her arms were just hanging naturally at her sides.

3. MAKE SURE THE PERSON IS ON THE SAME LEVEL THAT YOU ARE.

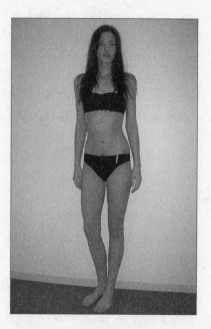

What a difference! Being on the same horizontal plane as the person who takes your picture is crucial—you will get the most realistic view of yourself for your audience, the modeling agencies. Also, make sure that the person holding the camera is flush to your face and body, and that he or she is not tilting the camera up or down in any way.

Now that your nonprofessional photographer knows what to do, let's concentrate on what *you* need to do!

PRACTICE, PRACTICE, PRACTICE

Practice different expressions in the mirror before you pose for these pictures. Smile at different intensities, furrow your brow, raise your eyebrows, pout, look into the mirror with no expression at all, and figure out how you can fill your face with energy, especially in your eyes. It is good to do face stretches, mainly from the mouth, right before the pictures are taken, in addition to practicing in front of the mirror, so you are more relaxed when you look at the camera. Open your mouth as wide as you can for a few seconds, then release. Some people tend to tighten up their mouth when they are nervous, and it is very easy for a professional to pick that out when looking at your pictures. Also, raise your eyebrows as high as you can for a couple of seconds, then release. You will subtly feel your face settle down. By practicing facial stretches and expressions in the mirror, you will observe certain facial movements that you never realized you had.

Another good way to practice is to have someone take digital photos of you so you can erase them easily. Make the same facial expressions into the digital camera that you practiced in the mirror. Observe how your facial movements translate onto film. Is your smile a little too broad sometimes? Then tone it down and try again. How about when you take a picture with your face relaxed. Are you *so* relaxed that there is a lack of energy in your eyes? There is a fine line between a look that is without obvious expression, and a look that is flat and dull. Figure out the difference by practicing and observing. Compare the different pictures with your various expressions.

Do you still feel nervous in front of a camera? Try closing your eyes a few seconds before the photographer is ready, then take a deep breath and let it out slowly. When the photographer says he or she is ready, open your eyes and have the photographer take the picture immediately. Try this a few times. It really makes a difference in the expression in the eyes, and makes the muscles in the face more relaxed. I worked with a lot of "real people" models who had never been in front of a camera for more than a family picture (especially in my position at *More* magazine), and this always seemed to help calm people down and get a great shot. I did it through my whole career in modeling and got some of the best shots that way. Try it with a digital camera, and see the difference.

After you experiment with the camera, get the opinion of another person. It's really difficult to be objective about your looks, and a third party will look at you more objectively, as an agency would. After you print the pictures, ask that person which expression he or she thinks is more captivating, what poses are more flattering, or what lighting shows the truest skin tones of your body. People love to give their opinions about things, especially something as fun as looking at modeling pictures. Who wouldn't want to help a potential model? Be careful though—your facial expressions and the way you stand are going to look different in a picture than in real life! Make sure you ask people's opinions about the way you are in your *pictures,* not the way you normally look to them in person.

YOUR BODY SHOT

For the bathing suit picture, females should stand with their legs together, feet pointed out front, and bend one leg at the knee slightly. The foot of the bent leg should be up on the ball of your foot, delicately balancing your bent leg so that you are not standing crooked or leaning to one side at all. This makes you look more elegant, with hands down naturally on both sides. Be careful not to bend the knee *too* much, because that will throw out your hip on the other side and make you look bigger, as well as more "posey" or unnatural. Males should stand with their feet shoulder-width apart, arms uncrossed, and have their hands to their sides as well, in a natural position.

Important for both males and females: Do not try to use your hands or arms to cover up any excess weight; you will not fool anyone! Also, do not lean against something or cheat your body to one side to try and hide something. That kind of body language is a telltale sign to an agent, and though you may think you are hiding something small, you will actually be doing the opposite, by inadvertently drawing attention to it.

When you are in a bathing suit (or any clothing, for that matter), throw your shoulders back and pull in your diaphragm while pulling up through your torso to make yourself look taller and longer. This stance drastically elongates your body and makes you appear slimmer! It also helps you exude a feeling of confidence. Don't overexaggerate the pose though; make it look as if you stand that way all the time naturally. Body language is *really* important in the modeling industry, because people are going to be "sizing you up" (no pun intended!) constantly. It is quite amazing what you can do with your posture to make yourself look more appealing. And remember these posture tips for when you meet some-one at a modeling agency—your body language will say it all.

YOUR HEAD SHOT

For the smiling head shot, do not force a smile. Try to think of some-thing really happy, such as your last vacation, your boyfriend or girl-friend, or perhaps imagine the moment when an agency says they want to sign you. Uncomfortable smiles are easy to detect in pictures, so practice until you become natural at it. Train your face how to smile easily and naturally . . . this all comes from practicing in front of the camera and observing yourself in the mirror.

For the pictures where you are not smiling, when you look at the camera, make sure you have some energy behind your eyes, as if you were on a photo shoot for *Vogue* magazine! Take a few pictures to practice, and see the difference. Try what I said before—close your eyes for a minute and then take a deep breath while the person who is taking the pictures gets the camera ready. Then, when he or she has a finger on the button to take your picture, open your eyes and look into the camera. This is especially effective on the unsmiling shots.

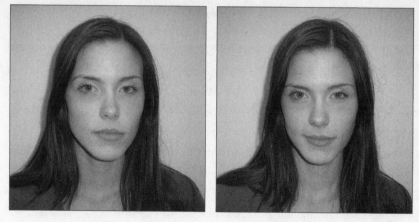

BEFORE   AFTER

Also, take a few pictures from exaggerated angles, from below as well as up above, to sort out what angle is best for you, and so that you can see the difference in the pictures for yourself.

VIDEO REQUESTS

If a foreign agency likes you, they may ask you for a video, because obviously they may not be meeting you in person before they sign you to their agency. Videos are done in much the same way as your digital or Polaroid pictures, keeping in mind the theme of simplicity with your makeup and clothing. Borrow a video camera if you do not have one, or if your phone takes videos, use that. Just keep in mind that if you send in something that is not that clear, the agency that requested a video may just turn you down instead of asking you for another one.

High-fashion requests. You will do the same thing for the video that you did in taking the pictures, such as showing all the angles of your face in the different shots with your hair up, hair down, etc., plus the body shots, but on videotape this time instead of as separate shots from a camera. You can also wear the same simple outfit, because the viewer will want to see more of *you,* not more of your closet. It can be one continuous video; you do not have to edit it. The only part that the camera will have to stop for is when you change into your bathing suit for the body shot. Say your name at the beginning, and then state your height, age, where you're from, and a phone number with an area code. Try to throw some personality in there as well, maybe a smile or a flirty look here and there when saying your name—whatever you are feeling at the time. There is so much competition in the fashion world that personalities count for a lot, especially in a videotape.

Since you are trying for a high-fashion agency, you will have to show them how you walk. Keep it natural, and refer to my tips for walking, in chapter 4. After you have said the introduction with your name, etc., turn around and walk slowly away from the camera for about six to eight paces, then turn around again, pause for a second facing the camera in the bathing suit pose that I described to you, with one leg slightly bent (you can use that bathing suit pose with clothes on as well as in your bathing suit), and walk back toward the camera with confidence. Then you can stop the camera, change into your bathing suit, and make sure the camera person films you from your head to your toes in your swimsuit.

Finish the video by again saying your name, height, age, and where you are from, then do not look away from the camera lens until the person who is filming you has turned off the camera.

Video requests for other categories. It's easy to videotape yourself after reading about the kinds of pictures I taught you how to take, because it is the same idea, except on video as opposed to film. It can be an amateur video, one that a friend of yours takes of you, and you should wear the same thing that you wore for the pictures. Say your name at the beginning, and then state your height, age, where you're from, and a phone number with an area code. Since you are not going for high fashion, this video clip needs to be a little more upbeat and personable, and you *do not need to walk* unless the agency specifically requested you to do so (tips for walking are in chapter 4). The commercial markets abroad like to see lots of smiles and personality, so after you state your name, etc., at the beginning, go ahead and say why you would like to go to whatever country to model, or talk about some of your hobbies or skills. Keep it short and sweet (about twenty to thirty seconds), and talk to the camera as if you were having a conversation with your best friend. Then, when you are done with the banter, turn off the camera for a minute to change into your swimsuit, and give a swimsuit pose (how I taught you to stand), with the camera person filming you from head to toe. You will finish the video by again saying your name, height, age, and where you are from. You should say all of this without looking away from the lens of the camera until the camera is turned completely off by the person who is filming you.

A MODEL SPEAKS OUT ABOUT THE STILL-POPULAR POLAROIDS AND/OR DIGITAL PICTURES

When I was an agent with Ford Models in New York City, Chantal Bolivar was one of my models. She is a gorgeous girl whose parents migrated from Guadeloupe Island in the Caribbean, then brought Chantal up in the suburbs of Paris. She came to New York City straight from France, and it was her first time modeling in the United States. Her portfolio was very substantial, as she had a lot of tear sheets and experience behind her from modeling in Europe, but she did not know how to take a Polaroid or digital picture! It was a totally different experience for her. "When I first walked into my former agency (Ford Models in New York) as a new model in New York City with Judy as my booker, she asked me if I knew how to take a Polaroid or digital picture. I really thought that I did! I had already modeled before and knew how to pose. Well, posing for a regular camera was *totally* different from taking a professional picture, and we ended up having a photo session right there in the hallway of her office so she could show me the difference."

Since coming to the States, Chantal has worked for Levi's, Gap, Nike, Maybelline, and L'Oréal advertising and campaigns. She has also worked for Saks Fifth Avenue, Macy's, and Bloomingdale's catalogs, and has appeared in various magazines around the world, including French *Elle, Glamour,* and *Essence* magazines.

I asked Chantal why (with her recent modeling experience) is it so important to know how to take Polaroid (or digital) pictures? And she answered "because every agency that you will go and see, as well as clients (when you start working as a model), will take Polaroid or digital pictures. There are certain angles that you have to know, and practicing is really important. Sometimes, clients will even base choosing the models off of digital pictures! And agencies will test you by taking these when they first meet you; if you know how to take a good Polaroid or digital picture, that is the first step to getting an agency. I was a model coming from Paris, and did not realize the *American market absolutely depends on Polaroid and digital pictures!* Nowadays people are taking more and more digitals, but I have even seen female models in a new-faces high-fashion division book *Vogue* magazine with just Polaroid pictures in their portfolio! This is rare, but it still happens, because agencies and clients look for raw talent, especially in the high-fashion sector."

What does Chantal feel is the best piece of advice for new models? "Do not ever spend money for professional pictures if you do not have an agency—it is a waste of time and especially money. And modeling schools may be great for pageants and other contacts, but they are not realistic in the everyday world of modeling. Remember, not everyone can be a model, and spending more and more money will not increase your chances of getting representation."

If you want to learn more about Chantal and what she is doing now, including her work as a VJ host, visit her Web site: www.chantal bolivar.com. Chantal is currently with Wilhelmina Models in New York City.

You heard it from a professional! It all takes practice and learning, and reading this book will help you learn how to do that. So many people have tried to get into the modeling industry by trial and error, and unfortunately that can be an e xpensive lesson to learn. Learning how to take the proper pictures without paying for them before you get into the industry can not only help you break in sooner, but will also aid you in the long run once you are with an agency. The experience is invaluable on so many different levels, and it is a major advantage to learn the basics of picture taking before you even enter the industry. After you know this you will already be a step ahead in your search for an agency, as well as in your future career as a model.

PROMOTION

Now that you have the perfect pictures in hand, are you ready to learn how to contact the right people? This is the exciting part—the beginning of the marketing process. It may have seemed a little tedious to learn the categories or figuring out the best angles for taking photos of yourself, but those steps are *absolutely crucial* in bringing you to this point. I want to make sure you are good and ready to step out into the modeling world when you introduce yourself for the first time. First impressions count!! Or, if you already tried to break into the industry before you read this book, try again my way and see what happens.

You see, modeling agencies do not care how they find a new face, that's why marketing yourself is so easy. Yes, they will open up an e-mail from an established manager or scout first, but that's why I am teaching you how to appear as if you know how to *manage yourself*—so agencies will pay attention to you and know you mean business!

This chapter gets really specific on how to narrow down the type of agency you should be marketing yourself to. It also goes deep into the heart of all the descriptions of models (yes, there are more!), and how to apply the modeling lingo to yourself. This information is important in helping you find the proper agency for your aesthetic type, as well as for your personality. When someone from an agency uses modeling lingo to describe your type of look, you will know what they are talking about after reading this chapter, and that will help you move forward with your search for representation.

The broadest approach, where you will reach the most people, is through mailing or e-mailing your pictures around the world to different agencies. There are specific looks for each market or city, as well as within the agencies of those cities. And within the agencies there are specific divisions to focus on for your mailings. Finally, in every division of an agency there are individual agents who will be looking at your pictures for possible representation. This pyramid shows the process.

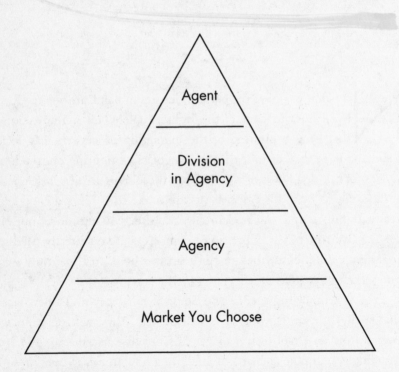

You want to try to get to the top of that pyramid for every mailing that you put together. At the very least, you should be able to get the name of a specific division (if the agency is large enough to house multiple divisions), if not the name of an agent along with that division. Just be careful not to cross the line of being *too* aggressive, because people will shut down and not help you if you push them too far and are overly demanding of their time. Always remember that they are doing *you* a favor while you are trying to find representation, and if you end up joining their agency, it will be the other way around—the agency will need to make *you* happy, because you are the reason they exist! Isn't that a wonderful thought . . . ?

Take Small Steps: Agencies in the United States

Larger cities will be a harder market to break into, because there is naturally more competition. So if you have access to a secondary market (smaller city or town) that is nearby, try that first, or at the very least at the same time you are trying to tap into the other markets. For example, if you live in Tampa, Florida, and are trying to get an agency in the Miami market, start selling yourself in the Tampa area first. There are a lot of great agencies to start you out in Tampa and help you eventually find your way into Miami. Then Miami can be a great stepping-stone to get your foot into the door of an agency in New York City. That is exactly how I personally got an agency in New York. People think that for some reason they can skip the step of starting in a secondary market by getting their own pictures taken by a professional photographer, putting a portfolio together themselves, and then bringing that portfolio into a highly competitive market like New York. The modeling industry does not work that way, besides it is a waste of money. Hopefully, you are catching on to that concept by now!

If local agencies in smaller markets love you—great! But do continue to send your pictures elsewhere, especially if you are in high fashion, before signing any contracts with anyone in a smaller market. You will not know the best choice for your personal career path if you do not explore all of your options. Don't get me wrong—smaller agencies can be a great way to build a career, as I just mentioned, but you might as well send your pictures to everyone you can, just to get their reaction.

Discovering an unrepresented great new face in the high-fashion industry is like striking gold to a big-time agency in New York City. I will teach you how to reach out not only in America but also around the world to modeling agencies for hardly any money, so you really should make the most of it.

If you live in a smaller market and you are not getting a good response from agencies there, could you possibly get into a prestigious agency in one of the larger, more highly competitive markets anyway? Of course—that's the exciting thing about the modeling industry! You never know where or when someone will discover you. You have to keep all of your feelers out and not limit yourself to any one market. You will most likely be traveling as a working model anyway, so starting out in another market as opposed to where you are from will give you good experience for the upcoming adventure. Once in a while high-fashion hopefuls *can* skip right to New York, Milan, or Paris, with just digital or Polaroid pictures, but do realize that the percentage of people who are able to do that is very small.

On the other hand, you could also be a superstar in a secondary market, make tons of money, and shoot for local ad campaigns, and then have trouble getting representation in a market such as New York or Europe. If this happens, most likely you are leaning toward a more commercial path as a model, and perhaps you should concentrate on targeting more *commercial agencies* in the bigger cities, or the more commercial markets that are located in other countries (which I will teach you about later on in this chapter).

What *is* the meaning of "commercial" model or "commercial market"? Well, one of the most important things you need to know about promoting yourself is that the entire modeling industry is broken up into two sections: editorial and commercial. You are either a more "editorial" model or a more "commercial" model—there is no way around it. And most markets lean either toward more "editorial" work or more "commercial" work. Some classifications are more obvious than others, such as a commercial print model being labeled as "commercial," but others are trickier in determining what type of model you are.

EDITORIAL VERSUS COMMERCIAL

Editorial models have unique facial characteristics, or they just have an overall more distinctive "look" about them, as compared to other models. It could be huge eyes, angular cheekbones, an interesting nose, or any combination of those and other unique features. Editorial models garner the attention of magazines and clothing designers more easily than commercial models do. They are often called "edgy" models in the fashion industry, and their measurements are often smaller than a typical model who is more commercial. Examples of high-fashion editorial models would be Linda Evangelista or Kate Moss. Both of these ladies do not have anything that can be considered "average" or "typical" about them.

Commercial models have more "classic" features (which I will describe right after this), or something in their look that is more approachable to the public eye. Great smiles with straight, white teeth are a big advantage in the commercial world. Now, don't get the term "commercial" confused with television "commercials," as television and film are a totally different entity from the modeling industry. I am strictly describing the print world; acting has its own standards to follow.

MORE ABOUT COMMERCIAL MODELS

Most potential models are going to tend to have a more "commercial" look about them, and that is another way of saying a more "mainstream" type of look. Commercial-looking models tend to fare better in commercial print, because their look has more mass appeal. Consumers find it easier to identify with a commercial model than they can with someone who is exotic or "different-looking." Commercial types are known in the industry as the more "approachable"-looking people. A female high-fashion model who is five eleven, 110 pounds, and drop-dead gorgeous in a very unique way (someone like Angelina Jolie), can sometimes be intimidating to a consumer and make it more difficult for the average person to relate to whatever product is being sold.

The term "commercial model" is one that is thrown around quite a bit in the modeling industry. I will explain in chapter 5 what it means when someone tells you that you are "too commercial" for their agency. This is usually a polite way of an agency turning you down, but don't forget that "commercial" models sometimes make the most money in the long run! So what sometimes seems like a put-down is often a compliment. If you want to know *how* commercial—ask! But be prepared for the truth. Someone may tell you to go into acting, that you would have a better chance in that industry than at modeling, but at least you will know and can target a new category or market, or possibly a whole new career. By the time you finish this book though, you will realize what to do with the different responses you get from modeling agencies, including when they say you are "too commercial." By the way, Elle Macpherson was considered to be a more "commercial" model, and she has made an incredible life for herself, including creating a globally successful lingerie company, Elle Macpherson Intimates. Not bad for a former swimsuit model!

These two classifications, "editorial" and "commercial," are an umbrella over the next breakdown I am going to teach you about. You will find out much more about yourself in the industry if you start throwing around the lingo—trust me! People will be impressed. Also, marketing yourself properly according to your specific look is crucial to your strategy of finding someone to represent you. The best way is to narrow down and get specific, just as we did with the inner framework of a modeling agency, and you will be able to be more specific only once you understand all these terms and their meanings.

Now that you understand about the "umbrella" of editorial versus commercial models, which covers the entire modeling industry, I am going to teach you about all the specific "looks" under that umbrella that are used in *both* the editorial and commercial classifications. Keep an open mind—these terms overlap here and there, and you could fall into more than one of the groups described.

You need to try and find out ahead of time what each agency is looking for in a potential model, not just what divisions an agency has. Modeling agencies have specific goals in mind of the kind of image they want to portray for the models they represent, and these descriptions will narrow it down for you even more. You will hear people, such as agents, throw around these terms to describe a particular type of look, or to let you know the kinds of models they are looking for at the moment, or to describe what type of models they currently represent. These terms are not to be confused with the requirements I gave you earlier in the category descriptions in chapter 1. The categories in chapter 1 should be chosen *first* according to their individual requirements, then these particular classifications will be used to narrow down your type of look within the category you chose.

Again, the following terms are more broad and subjective than other descriptions I have given you about how to classify what type of model you are. I will give you an example later on, so that you will be able to tie it all together.

- **Classic features.** Having a more "classic" look means smaller facial features (more delicate), clean and fresh-looking skin, healthy hair, and a nice smile with straight teeth. Classic-looking models tend to lean toward a more commercial career in modeling, although you can be labeled as "classic" under the editorial side of modeling too, it's just not as common. The typical example of a designer who uses classic types of models is Ralph Lauren. This type of model could be the girl or boy next door; approachable but still beautiful.
- **Exotic faces.** This can be anything from ethnic-looking to a captivating beauty with hard-to-pinpoint origins. An exotic model can be editorial or commercial. Eva Mendes is a perfect example of an "exotic" look, along with Angelina Jolie. These two celebrities are completely different-looking, yet they both fall under the "exotic" description in the modeling world.
- **Unique facial characteristics.** Exotic and unique types overlap (I *told* you these descriptions are hard to precisely pinpoint), but when someone tells you that you are "unique," it's probably because you have a specific facial characteristic or other quality that makes your overall look more definitive. The word "unique" more commonly describes editorial models. An example of unique look is Linda Evangelista.

- **Ethnic.** This one is pretty self-explanatory, but the thing you should know is that if you fall into the "ethnic" category, you probably don't have much of a crossover for other types of looks in the modeling world. In other words, if an agency or client is looking for "exotic" or "classic" models, "ethnic" models would not automatically be included in that request unless it specified "all ethnicities." The term "ethnic" is used when you can quickly pinpoint where a model is from, or what nationality he or she represents, if the description of Caucasian is not an option. If someone is from a few different backgrounds but is still technically "ethnic," it is translated differently in the modeling industry, and that model is open to more opportunities, not being restricted to one nationality. For example, if you can immediately see that someone is of Asian or African descent, like Alec Wek, he or she will be considered strictly "ethnic." Latin models can go both ways, because some people with Latin backgrounds cross over into Caucasian characteristics aesthetically, like supermodel Gisele. She does an impressive job of representing *all kinds* of models— from *Vogue* to Victoria's Secret. I consider her to be the ultimate adaptable model in the twenty-first century.

MORE ABOUT ETHNIC MODELS

If you are of African or Asian descent, or are not considered to be "Caucasian," there are certain markets that may be more receptive to your type of look. Send your pictures wherever you want, of course, but I would like to give you an idea of what markets may work out better for your type of look (another example of my "target marketing" concept).

First of all, America is more open to ethnic models in their advertising than any other market in the world. New York City is your best bet, but New York is also the hardest market to break into as a new model, so it's a double-edged sword. Even so, start with the United States, especially the larger cities (because you *never* know), then Milan would be a good second choice to send your pictures. London is another market that is more open to ethnic models, but you should still keep yourself open to other markets as well. The more "commercial" markets that I write about later in this chapter would probably be your last choice of where to try to break into the modeling industry as an ethnic model, because these markets predominantly use Caucasian models. But if you have lighter skin, and are either a mix ethnically or are more "all-American"-looking with classic features, then definitely send your pictures to commercial markets as well.

There *is* less work for ethnic models on the whole, but that shouldn't stop you from marketing yourself to whomever you can. Just be strategic about it, listen to what people are saying about your type of look, and go after it. The advantage is, if an ethnic model *does* make a name for himself or herself in the modeling industry, he or she has the possibility of going beyond what other models can do in the long run. Tyra Banks, Naomi Campbell, Iman, and Kimora Lee Simmons have opened many doors for minorities to become successful in the modeling industry. Those four are just some of the examples of "non-Caucasian" models who have reached supermodel status and have maintained their supermodel label over the years, in addition to delving into other industries with their multifaceted talents. Ethnic looks can be trendy as well, so one season the fashion world may not be leaning toward your look, and another season everyone may be searching for ethnic girls or guys.

Chantal Bolivar, the girl from Paris that I interviewed earlier in chapter 2, is of African descent. She did exceptionally well for herself in America and moved into television work as well! So don't get discouraged when I tell you there is less work—if you have a great look and a personality to go with it, you should go far. Chantal did, even though when she first arrived in the United States she did not start working immediately. But she stuck it out and listened to her agent, and eventually she created a successful career for herself.

Models who are of a Latin background ride the wave of being both "Caucasian" and "Ethnic." When I was a modeling agent and I got a call for Caucasian models, the client usually wanted to see Latin-based models as well. When I got a request for *ethnic* models, the client would most often be specific, asking for models of Latin, Asian, or African descent, or they might specify wanting someone who looked "ethni-cally ambiguous." Those of you out there who are not easily classifiable as one ethnicity know who you are!

I personally happen to dislike labeling people (especially by race), but it cannot be ignored in the fashion industry, since the whole business is based on looks, and you need to fully understand where *your* look is going to be best represented. In the end you can only be yourself, so whatever your background, just go for it with the same determination that everyone else does and please do not get turned off or offended by the labels.

SWIMSUIT OR FITNESS MODELS

A bathing beauty can be classic, exotic, unique *or* commercial! Con-fused yet? I added this description type because there are many guys and girls out there who do not have the height for fashion modeling but have a great face and body, and will be told that you "would be good for bathing suit (or fitness) modeling." There isn't a *huge* market out there for this kind of model, but there is money to be made if you specialize in this genre. In the warmer states there tend to be more clients who regularly book for swimwear and fitness, but in other regions there are agencies that specialize in these types of models also, like Silver Model Management in New York City. Topher DésPrés, director of Silver Model Management, states that "a common misconception among as-piring swimsuit and/or fitness models is that bigger and leaner is better. The facts are that before a model can work successfully as a fitness model, they need to appear healthy, and being healthy doesn't constitute extremely low body fat percentages or overly large muscles. In fact, a successful fitness model usually reminds us of a runner, swimmer, dancer, or the average person who regularly goes to the gym."

The marketing process is the same; you still have to do your re-search and call agencies to find out if they book bathing suit work, or have a body/fitness division. Start by sending your pictures to Silver Models, if New York is an option for you! Their contact information is in the back of this book. If you are pursuing this type of work, the only thing I would change is one of the *non*-smiling head shots that I told you to take in chapter 2. Substitute it with one in which you have a sexier expression if you are a female going after bathing suit work.

FINDING THE NAMES OF *ALL* TYPES OF MODELING AGENCIES

You can start with the agencies whose composites are shown in chapter 1, under "Categories of Modeling." I tried to select agencies from all over, so there would be something for everyone. Each agency's contact information is in the back of this book, including their Web sites, so you can check out all of their divisions. *Remember, just because a modeling agency calls itself "high fashion" or "talent" doesn't mean they don't have other divisions!* A good example is Ford Models in New York City. They are a "high-fashion" modeling agency yet have all kinds of other divisions, such as commercial print, plus size, fit, kids, and more. You need to do your research and go on the modeling agencies' Web sites to figure out if an agency has a division that is appropriate for your type to send your pictures to for consideration.

After you go through my handpicked list in chapter 1, the next way to find a modeling agency in your hometown (or any other town for that matter) is to use a search engine on the computer and put in "model agency," then the next word should be the town in which you are trying to find an agency. For example, if I were searching for agencies in Nashville, Tennessee, I would go to www.google.com, and put in "model agency nashville." The agencies pop right up and you can find phone numbers, addresses, URLs, and maps.

Another way to search names is to go to www.models.com, and get an agency's contact information from their Web site. Models.com is an excellent resource for information on modeling agencies as well as up-to-date news on models and the different markets around the world.

If you don't mind spending a little bit of money to get a directory sent to you, then order the "Model and Talent Directory" from PG Direct. Their Web site is www.pgdirect.com. Most modeling agencies use this resource for contacting agencies around the world, but it is sometimes outdated before the next version is printed, so you will find agencies in there that have moved or are out of business. On the other hand, if you search on the Internet and a modeling agency is out of business, their Web site is usually taken down, so you can know immediately if a particular agency is no longer functioning.

BOUTIQUE AGENCIES

Smaller agencies, sometimes called "boutique" agencies, can be power-houses, and a good lead-in for other markets, as well as a good way to learn the business before you jump into a mammoth city like New York or Los Angeles. And if you already live in a big city and want to start your marketing there, boutique agencies also have advantages when they are located in larger cities. Usually you get more personal attention from a smaller agency, and the relationship can feel more as if you are a member of a family. It depends what you are looking for both professionally and personally.

Rosie Niku is the owner of a high-fashion boutique agency in Beverly Hills called Bleu Model Management. Rosie feels that "although Los Angeles might not be the fashion capital of the world, it certainly is the breeding ground of many beautiful models. Attempting to fulfill the hopes and dreams of every young person from around the world with its glitz and glamour of Hollywood, Los Angeles has been and always will be a great scouting region. With its many facets of entertainment, this city is a great place to start a young model's career, as there is less competition than in the main markets, such as New York and Europe. On the one hand, the pace is slower and less stressful, not only allowing a model to create a great portfolio but also preparing him or her for the chaotic world of high fashion. On the other hand, it is an excellent choice for a final destination with the more established models, as they frequently pursue careers in acting. Either way, whether a model is trying to break new ground or just ready to trade in their stilettos for acting classes, LA is a great place to be."

If you would like to send pictures into Bleu Model Management, you have to meet the high-fashion requirements. The agency's contact information is in the back of this book; Bleu Model Management is a legitimate, reputable modeling agency, and if you feel that Los Angeles is an option for you, start there!

Smaller agencies usually also specialize in one type of model (such as high fashion, men, fitness, plus sizes, etc.), so clients know that when they call a more modest-size agency they will get fewer models to choose from, but there is more of a chance that every model proposed to them will be specifically tailored to their needs. Also, at the smaller agencies, sometimes the agents worked for years at a larger agency, and they have all of the same contacts for clients, like Ray Volant from Bella Agency in New York City. He was the director of the Ford Models NY commercial print division for eight years, then he opened his own agency specializing in commercial print. As a client, when I call larger agencies for models, I sometimes get inundated with too many proposals, which can become quite overwhelming. As a model you also may feel that the larger agencies can be overwhelming, or you may like the anonymity a larger agency brings; it all depends on your personality.

WITHIN A MODELING AGENCY

Now that I have shown you how to narrow down the different markets and kinds of agencies for your look, let's now focus on finding a *specific division* along with a *specific person*'s *name* to whom you can send your mailings. Get specific, because agencies will open a letter much faster if there is a name or a division written on the envelope. General mail to an agency has about a 50 percent chance of being looked at for more than a quick second (a higher percentage for smaller agencies), so singling out an agent or at least a division if you can't get a name is always a good idea, especially for the larger agencies. Agencies periodically check info@ mailboxes because no one wants to miss a great potential new face, but an e-mail to a specific agent has more of a chance of being seen, and there is even more of a chance that your pictures will be scrutinized more closely. I personally made sure that all of the general e-mail addresses you see in Contact Information in the back of this book are being checked constantly—some of the owners even check it themselves!

Notice I said *try* to get the name of an agent . . . that is because it isn't always that easy to get the names of people working at an agency, because of privacy issues. If the receptionist won't connect you to an agent, try to call back the next day and get more information out of him or her—they won't remember who you are, or recognize your voice. Every agent is usually on the phone all day, for hours at a time, especially the receptionist. The best time to call is around ten in the morning (after everyone has had their coffee), or about three in the afternoon (before people wrap up their days). If you call at other times, you could get hungry people who have lost their patience (right before lunch), or simple chaos (after four) when modeling agencies get overly hectic with models checking in for their appointments and jobs for the next day, and clients calling with last-minute requests for an agent before the end of the workday.

Hint: when calling an agency (especially the smaller ones), ask the person who answers the phone if they are a "booker" *first,* before you say anything else. If they are, they will let you know before asking you who you are. Smaller agencies often do not have receptionists, so it is easier to get through to an agent on the phone. You see, when a model starts rambling on the phone about wanting to get into the modeling industry, some agents (okay, most agents), turn their hearing off on the side that the phone receiver is on, or quickly pass the potential model on to a voice-mail recording that tells you either where to send your pictures, or about their open calls. If you ask the person right off the bat if they are an agent, you may have their attention for a few seconds and then be able to ask a question. Another tip is to simply ask for whatever division you need without saying who you are, and you may get connected directly to an agent without getting the third degree from the receptionist. Don't be vague—select one question and ask it right away if you get on the line with an agent. Be assertive, but *not aggressive.*

If you are a potential candidate for the high-fashion category, try asking the agency for their "new-faces" or "scouting" division, and if you get connected with someone, ask them their name so you can include it when addressing the envelope with your pictures. If someone who is already employed by an agency spots you, there is no fee or concerns about percentages being shared for placement within that agency. Let me explain . . . a lot of agencies have scouts on their staff placed there solely to find new faces. A scout who has his or her own company (as a freelance scout), and wants to place you with an agency, will charge that agency a fee, and/or a percentage of your income. It is not such a terrible thing, but if you are an unattached model approaching an agency without a manager, scout, or mother agency, it makes you that much more attractive to an agency.

COMMERCIAL PRINT HINT

If the commercial print category is calling your name, here's a tip for you: many "commercial" agencies (as in television commercials) book commercial print jobs as well, and have divisions specializing in it. Also look for modeling agencies that are labeled as "model and talent" as opposed to "model management" companies. Commercial print is a *huge* industry that includes a broad range of people, so this will be one of the easier divisions to target. This is much less competitive than high fashion, because of the influx of "real"-looking people who more and more companies are using in their advertising. Don't get me wrong—it's still very competitive, but at a lesser scale than high fashion.

PUTTING IT ALL TOGETHER

So, let's try to make some sense out of all the information and descriptions in this chapter. If you haven't already selected a category from chapter 1 based on my descriptions of the physical requirements that are listed, go back and do this before moving on. Remember, the requirements in the first chapter under each category are *not* negotiable. Age and size requirements are the strictest and should be closely observed.

After you figure out your category, and whether you are more "editorial" or more "commercial," you will start to realize what "type" of model you are by the descriptions I just explained to you. Do you have any unique facial features? Or are you the type of person who has more classic features? Do people see you as more exotic? All these terms describe models under both editorial and commercial groupings.

Don't forget, these are subjective labels, so keep an open mind. One person may see you as classic, and someone else may come along and describe you as more exotic. Do not fret! Everyone has a different way of looking at people, and you should be pushing for both of those descriptions when marketing yourself, if that's what you start hearing from professionals in the modeling industry. Supermodel Gisele can be commercial, bathing suit, and editorial all at the same time! *Don't change who you are, or change your pictures!* Just send your pictures to two different divisions within one agency, if it seems like your look covers both and you pass the requirements in both of the categories that I originally listed in chapter 1. Also send your pictures to two different *agencies* that have each of the looks you believe you fall under. Expand your search while still being specific—that's why I am teaching you about the characteristics of different modeling agencies and how to find out the type of model they are looking for, as well as what image an agency is trying to portray.

Let me give you an example of how to get the most out of your search. If I went to a few open calls for high fashion, and agents or scouts kept telling me I was either too "commercial" (which most people will hear quite a bit) or had a look that was very "classic," I would ask the person right then and there (who is hosting the open call) if they had a more commercial division that would see me that very same day. Nothing wrong with trying to get more people to see you in person!! In fact, that's what being a manager is all about—getting yourself as much exposure as you can. And if they did not have anyone else available to see me in *their* agency, I would then ask if they could give me the name of someone else in that same agency in one of the more commercial divisions, or if they could suggest a more commercial agency I could contact. After that, I would then send my pictures to more commercial agencies and people working in commercial print at the same time that I was looking for a high-fashion agency. I would also attend any open calls for more commercial-type agencies or divisions. Don't be stubborn and restrict yourself to limited options, because you may see yourself in a totally different market than what you really are. *You* may think you look like Gisele, but fashion industry professionals may see you completely different, and it is in your best interest to listen to what they have to say and market yourself appropriately.

When you are your own manager, you need to market yourself just as a manager would, and try every angle at your disposal. That is why it is good to learn the lingo and all the descriptions you can, so when you are listening to someone critique you, you can not only understand what they are trying to say, but also possibly ask a question or two to help you move forward, instead of trying to figure out what they are saying and meanwhile losing the chance to get more valuable information. People in the fashion industry move very fast, and if you are not quick enough, you may lose your chance to obtain valuable information from someone in person.

Do you feel as if you are ready to try your hand at overseas representation? Modeling overseas presents a great opportunity for starting your career. Europe and other foreign markets are sometimes more open to new faces, especially in the high-fashion category. Foreign markets also present good opportunities for other types of models as well, primarily women's and men's main fashion. The next section will give you a good idea of how the foreign markets work—they are easier to access than you think.

European and Other Foreign Markets

New faces in Europe are more readily accepted by modeling agencies because they are known for taking more risks on beginners. Plus, they have the same requests for nonprofessional pictures as the agencies in *this* country do! And you do not have to speak the language—foreign agencies are used to Americans who only speak English. So it's easy to include the foreign market in your search for representation. The only difference is that agencies from overseas may ask you to send a video of yourself in addition to the Polaroid or digital pictures, which I covered how to take in chapter 2.

The most important thing about looking for representation overseas is to make sure the agency is legitimate. Usually the ones that will advance you plane fare, hotel, and test pictures for your portfolio mean business, but check out their Web site and ask them for references from other agencies anyway.

If they won't advance airfare and accommodations, make sure you ask if they will at least advance money for composites and test pictures for your portfolio. Don't *expect* any money or financial help in advance, it doesn't happen to everyone. But there is no harm in trying! If an agency wants you badly enough, they may contribute more money than you think. You see, agencies know they have to invest a certain amount of money in potential new faces to possibly gain a working model or maybe a superstar, so they understand that people need help when beginning their careers. It takes a lot of money to get started in a foreign country, and a new model may not be making a profit right away. Advances happen more often within the world of high fashion, but you can find agencies who are willing to help in other categories as well, at the very least by advancing for pictures and composites, which you will have to agree to pay back at a later date, when you start work-ing for them. If you do not make enough money to pay back the agency *and* survive at first, then an agreement can be worked out where you get a certain percentage of your earnings, and the agency gets the rest until you pay back your debt. *Everything is negotiable,* if an agency really wants you.

You should *always* ask for financial help if a foreign modeling agency is interested in you; the worst they can say is no! It won't change their opinion of you, I promise. It may even impress agencies about your business savvy and will make them aware that you know what you are doing. Your best bet is to ask for an advance for accom-modations *before* you get there, and/or plane fare to get you there and back. A lot of times the agencies will have models' apartments or dis-counts on hotels, and I go further into detail about this in chapter 7. But no matter how much money a modeling agency will advance you, please be sure to check them out thoroughly *before* going overseas.

Be prepared to spend at least two months in a foreign market by the time you test with photographers, make a portfolio with new pictures, select the pictures to use with composites, see clients, and wait for your agency to sell you to clients in that market after you meet them in per-son on castings. Some markets work faster than others, and other markets take more time to obtain steady work. I have known people to be in Europe for six months or more without working a whole lot, and then when the momentum begins, they end up working like crazy. It takes time in *any* market for most new models to get a career going, so you have to have a lot of patience and invest time as well as money.

EDITORIAL FOREIGN MARKETS

Milan, Paris, London, Madrid, and Athens will all take chances on new, as well as unique or exotic faces, but usually only in the high-fashion category. Milan is probably your best bet, because they love to take on brand-new faces, and there is a wide range of looks they will consider, especially if you're in that "unique"- or "exotic"-looking genre, as opposed to a "classic" look. These are some of the terms I just taught you . . . did you recognize them? If not, go back and memorize them if you want to be in this business, because the more you know and understand, the further you will get in your search for representation.

An expert on the modeling industry in Europe, Angelo Laudisa was a former model agency director for five years at Why Not Agency in Milan, Italy, then went on to become director of Ford Models in Paris for eight years before starting his new company, Talents Europe Management (TEM) in Paris. TEM manages high-profile sports stars, actors, and musicians in Europe, artfully bringing celebrities together with both the fashion world and product advertising. Here are some thoughts from Mr. Laudisa regarding the modeling industry in Milan, Italy.

"Milan is a very good market for high-fashion beginning models, which is one of the reasons why Italy is one of the world's foremost leaders in fashion. Located within Milan, the head offices of well-known Italian designers such as Armani, Prada, Versace, Dolce & Gabbana, and Roberto Cavalli are situated there.

"If a reputable agency *does* ask you to come to Italy but is not able to pay for anything in advance for you, it's a good idea to try and invest your money into this market as a beginning model anyway. Try to work out (with the interested agency) some advances for testing and composites, and see what happens. The world of modeling is about taking risks! But be aware—the city of Milan can be hectic, with people always moving around very fast, so make sure you are ready for the change of pace if you are from a small town. If you survive the Milano experience as a model, then you are sure to be more prepared for bigger scenarios in your modeling career, like Paris and New York City."

Mr. Laudisa also suggests that if you want to model in Italy, you should try these selected agencies first (see below). Some of them are smaller than others, but in his opinion they are all great agencies and have a highly regarded reputation after decades of being in the modeling business.

Beatrice Models: www.beatricemodels.it
Fashion Models: www.fashionworld.it
Women Management: www.womenmanagement.it

I have worked with all of the agencies listed above both as an agent and a model at some point in my career. If any of them want you to come to Italy to start your modeling career, it is a great opportunity with a reputable agency, and you should try your best to go. Each of these agencies' e-mail addresses to send pictures to is in Contact Information in the back of this book, or better yet, go on their Web sites first to check them out.

Again, if you are not referred to an agency but one of them that you know nothing about is interested in representing you, make sure the agency is legitimate *before* boarding any planes or *giving out any personal information*. I cannot stress to you enough to do your research and follow up on *all* of the references given to you and what they have to say about the agency you are considering. This is especially important when considering companies that are located in foreign countries.

COMMERCIAL MARKETS

If you are not in the high-fashion category, some of the agencies that are more open to commercial looks overseas are Australia, Germany, Greece, Switzerland, Austria, and Japan. These markets have been known to take more commercial-looking models, and there is the potential to make a good amount of money in these countries as well. Agencies usually invest more money in younger high-fashion hopefuls, but if you send your pictures to these markets and they really like you, you may be able to negotiate at least an advance for plane fare and accommodations.

Most foreign modeling agencies will advance tests, pictures, and composites once you arrive, but make sure to confirm that before you go. If the agency won't advance you money before you get there, make sure you ask how much a place to stay would be (agencies usually have lodging deals for models), and find out the price of a round-trip ticket and how much spending money you would need to live there. If an agency overseas likes you and they *can't* advance you money or a plane ticket, you should think about investing in yourself if you have the funds. Believe me—a reputable modeling agency is not going to take you on for no reason; they want you because they think they can get work for you! This is especially true in the more commercial markets, where models tend to start working quicker than in an editorial market.

Germany is one of the markets that have a consistent need for a specific type of commercial model. The clients have a specific look that they use over and over again—classic, healthy appearance, with a beautiful smile and radiant skin. If you are the type of model their clientele demands, you will start working right away and can acquire a steady flow of work very quickly. German catalogs and advertising clients tend to be very loyal, so repetitive work for these models is quite common.

Also, the magazines in Germany are a little more commercial than the ones in Italy or France, which means that they prefer a more mainstream type of look, and the kind of editorial work in Germany pays more than in any other country. Plus if you work for the magazines in this market, you have more of a chance of the German catalog and advertising clients booking you as well, which can provide significant income.

Founded in 1971 and located in Hamburg, Germany, Model Team is a great example of the kind of reputable agency where a new model can start his or her career in a commercial market overseas. Not only is

Model Team the oldest modeling agency in Germany, but it is also one of the most successful to date. Soni Ekvall, founder and president of Model Team, shares with us a few words on breaking into the modeling business as a new model in Germany.

"To start as a model in Hamburg is a really good move. The city is big enough to practice how to find clients, photographers, magazine editors, etc., when going on appointments, but still small enough so that the models can learn the city quickly and do not get lost. Model Team is like a big family, so all of the bookers take good care of the models, and there is always someone approachable for the younger girls. Also, having a models' apartment situated right next to our agency helps, so that models who are new to the city (or new to Europe) can feel more secure when first starting a modeling career."

When I asked Soni what her one piece of advice for new models might be, she added this message: "One of the most important concerns in this industry is to be on time!" And she's right—a model who is late for an appointment can be perceived as potentially being late to a job, and that could hurt his or her chances of getting work. You see, the appointment you go on when you meet clients is like a "tryout" from the client's perspective. If you can't be on time to an appointment, why should the client think that you are going to be on time to their photo shoot? Models who are late to work cost the whole production money, as well as stress, and no one wants to be a part of that kind of irresponsibility. The same rule goes for when you are meeting a modeling agency. If you are late for an appointment to see an agency for representation, then they might conclude that you are the type of model who is always late, and may embarrass the agency when you are sent on appointments. Modeling agencies spend a lot of time trying to get their models to see clients, even sometimes when the clients don't want to see anyone, and it is a huge waste of time for everyone when these appointments are not taken seriously.

You can find out more about Soni's agency online, at www.model team-hamburg.de, or see Contact Information in the back of this book. The e-mail is "info@", but Soni assured me your pictures *will* be seen by an agent. Send your pictures if you are interested in going to Europe! You never know if they will like you or not if you don't try. I am giving the more commercial-looking guys and gals a great contact to utilize, so please take advantage of it. And remember, Model Team *is* a high-fashion agency, but they are one of the modeling agencies that have other divisions as well, including plus-size models! So be sure you choose your category and market yourself correctly before sending your pictures.

Other reputable agencies in Germany to send your pictures to, that I personally recommend, are:

Okay Models in Hamburg: www.okaymodels.com
Nova Models in Munich: www.nova-models.de
Harry's Models in Munich: www.harrys-models.com

Look for their e-mail addresses to send pictures to in Contact Information at the back of this book, but also go on their Web sites to see what kind of models they are looking for, and the size of each agency.

A PERSONAL EUROPEAN STORY TO LEARN FROM

When I was a newer model, at one point I got sent to Germany to see clients. I had been in Milan and did not work for three months straight, and my Italian agency thought it would be good for me to make some money quickly to pay my bills, since Germany is typically a great commercial market and I seemed to be the type German clients liked. Then, they reasoned, I could come back to Milan after saving some money and keep trying to get the editorial that I needed to further my career in New York. This is part of the process I was trying to explain to you in chapter 1, about the path of a typical high-fashion model. It involves intense traveling, and the constant investment of money, sometimes for long stretches at a time.

Anyway, I arrived in Germany at night by train for the first time, not being able to speak the language and having no foreign currency on me (only lire from Italy—at that time the euro did not exist), to find that the hotel I was supposed to be staying at was locked up for the night! Hotels are not known for having twenty-four-hour service in Europe, like in America. The only other place (that I could see in the darkness from where I was standing) to stay overnight was the inn down the street, and I quickly found out by going over there that they did not take credit cards. The sweet lady running the inn that I had wandered into told me that the next day was a bank holiday, so I could not change my money then either, nor go into the agency for any kind of help because they would be closed. What did I do? I burst into tears, rolled my huge suitcase, which I couldn't even pick up, to a lighted phone booth, and called my boyfriend "collect" in America, sobbing hysterically. The woman from the inn down the road was watching my pathetic scene, had pity on me, and took me inside her hotel. While she served me some hot tea to calm my nerves, she told me I could pay her later on in the week when I finally got some money.

After that day I got smart—I changed some of my money into the currency of the country I was traveling to *before* I left for anywhere overseas. I also started packing a suitcase that I could pick up without assistance, in case there was no one around to help me. You live and learn, but it can be very stressful. I hope the modeling business will be less stressful on *you* though, now that you are reading this book and learning from my mistakes!

The flip side of that story is that Germany eventually went on to be my highest moneymaking country in the world. After I saw all the clients in Germany, I went back to the States and got booked through my German agency for jobs all over the world. I got to see the globe while making money. I eventually lived in Milan for almost a year, and also lived in cities such as Munich, Hamburg, São Paulo, New York City, and Miami Beach, all financed by my modeling career.

MORE REASONS TO TRY EUROPE

Another reason for marketing yourself in Europe is because agencies in cities like New York, Miami, and Los Angeles will most likely send you to Europe to build your portfolio anyway. This is very common and almost unavoidable for the high-fashion candidates, and for some of the other high-fashion categories as well. Commercial print and the other categories rarely have to travel to build their books.

New York is the most difficult market in the world to work in as a model, and American clients mostly like to see a girl who has worked in Europe first. Models go to foreign markets mainly to build a portfolio of tear sheets from magazines ("tear sheets" are the pictures of yourself you "tear" out of magazines for your portfolio) and put the pages in their books, to get more work in the States. If you do not get representation with an American agency to market yourself overseas, you can target the foreign clients the *same way* you are doing the marketing for the agencies in the United States—just make sure you thoroughly research their reputations, since you are going to be in foreign territory over there. Get referrals from agencies in the United States, and contact models who are already represented by the agency you are thinking about joining. Any legitimate agencies that want to sign you on as a model will be more than happy to prove their capabilities and reputation.

A WARNING ABOUT ALL AGENCIES

If you approach the wrong division within an agency, they will not consider you at all, and they usually will not bother to refer you to another division. They will just turn you down, and you will have lost one of your chances to succeed with that agency. Agents do not have the time or inclination to be "coaches" to people who are not signed with them, so that is why I am teaching you how to take charge of yourself with your own career and *be specific*. You will have the knowledge of how this industry works after reading this book, so use it in marketing yourself.

And once again, do not give out personal identification information such as your birth date, Social Security number, or anything else through e-mail or over the phone. Wait until you have established an agency's credibility. No one needs to know this kind of information *before* you start working with an agency.

Mailing Your Photos

Now you're ready to put your envelope together for your perspective agencies!

Before you waste money and time on printing, think about how you would like to present yourself, and present a consistent image in all the mailings you send to agencies. For example, if you decide to send glossy photos from a pharmacy photo developer to prospective agencies, then stick with that method. Organization is the key here, especially after you have worked so hard to figure out what type of model you are, and what agencies may be interested in your look. If you start sending out different kinds of mailings all different ways, it will be hard to decipher in the end what you can improve upon. For instance, let's say you sent out glossy pictures to one agency, color lasers to another agency, and Polaroid pictures to yet another agency. What happens if one of those agencies calls you back and says, "Could you send more of the same kind of pictures that you took, but just put on a different outfit?" You won't know which type of pictures they are talking about if your mailings weren't consistent.

If you want to make color laser copies, arrange what photos you would like to copy on each sheet of paper *before* you get to the color printing store and keep the original in case you need to go back to make more copies. Plus, sometimes if you go back to the photo or color laser place for additional prints and do not have the original setup, it will cost you more money because of setup or layout fees.

Do you have a color printer at home? Great! First test your copies out on regular copy paper (not photo paper) before printing a number of color copies. Photo paper can be expensive, and if you make a mistake, it should be on regular paper. You do not *have* to use photo paper if you want to save money; it just makes a nicer presentation.

Please don't Photoshop, color correct, retouch, or alter the photos you took in any way. If an agent sees you in person and is expecting something different because you doctored your photos, it will only get them upset. Sometimes models *do* retouch their pictures, but that is when he or she is more established in the business—a completely different scenario than trying to break into the business.

PUTTING TOGETHER YOUR MATERIALS TO SEND

1. Print out copies of your pictures, using one of the printing methods I described above. If you make color laser copies, put more than one photo on a page to save money, and also to make it more convenient for someone to see you all at once.

2. No more than *seven* pictures should be placed in the envelope (the ones I taught you how to take of course), with your name, phone number, age, height, measurements, sizes, hair color, eye color, and the city where you live on *every* picture, in case they get separated. Agents like to pass the pictures around the office when they find someone they like; therefore, your pictures *will* get separated. Four pictures on one color laser sheet and three on the other to make two sheets of pictures for an agent to see is perfectly acceptable—sometimes even preferred! If you are sending single pictures, paper clip them or staple them together, with the nonsmiling head shot on top of the pile for the high-fashion divisions, and a smiling one on top for the other categories.

3. Include a *very* short cover letter just requesting the agent or manager to look at your pictures, and then thank them for their time. Always put in the cover letter that you would appreciate any advice they can give, if they happen to have time to call you or write you back (not likely). A self-addressed stamped envelope may help, with questions on a separate piece of paper that you think will help you evaluate yourself—but don't include too many though, or they will not bother. Do not assume they will or will not be interested in you, just keep the questions neutral. For example, one of the questions could be: "Do you think your agency is right for me?" And another question could be: "Do you think I

have potential as a high-fashion (or whatever category you choose) model?" Then put boxes for them to check, either yes or no, so you make it really easy for them. And don't forget the self-addressed stamped envelope *inside* the envelope you are using to send your pictures. The easier you make it for someone to respond to you, the more chance you have of someone responding. Even if they don't send your pictures back and you get some sort of response from the self-addressed envelope, at least you will know someone saw your pictures. Of course, you can also go the more traditional route and send the pictures "return receipt request" from a post office, but that can be costly if you are sending pictures to more than just a few agencies. I hope you are going to find *many* agencies to send your pictures to, the more the better, as long as they are strategically selected.

4. Select the size envelope you want to use, and see if Staples or another office supply store or Web site will sell them to you cheaply or in bulk. Larger envelopes tend to make people more curious, but standard-size envelopes will do just as well.

5. At the bottom of the envelope write the name of one of the bookers at the agency and "Attention to" before that person's name. If you don't have someone's name to put on the bottom of the envelope, at least put the title "director" on it: "Attention: Director of High Fashion" or "Attention: Director of Commercial Print," and so on. You will have a better chance of someone opening your envelope—trust me.

E-mailing Your Photos

Worldwide Web—nothing beats it. Digital marketing of your pictures is the cheapest and easiest way to get noticed by an agent or manager. The modeling industry has made great strides in embracing digital technology: models' pictures are scanned into an agency's database to be put on the agency's Web site. Agencies can then make laser copies whenever they need to, without even having to use the original print from a photo shoot, and agencies also create digital portfolios to send to clients, like global advertising agencies who mainly work off of their computers. Fewer and fewer clients want to see the "hard copy" of models' portfolios, and clients prefer to at least do the preliminary casting for their product from digital pictures.

Because of the changeover from paper copies of pictures to digital images in the modeling industry, agents and managers can be very receptive to pictures by e-mail. Usually on the agency's Web site they have an address "info@soandsoagency.com," where someone will periodically check for new talent, but do try to get an individual's e-mail address. Sometimes agencies (especially the larger ones) get *countless* submissions of pictures in the general e-mail address, and they are looked at too quickly. Check on the back page of an agency's Web site, where they often list the bookers' names who work in the agency along with their e-mail addresses. Then you will have a specific person to whom you can send your pictures. Also it will make your follow-up easier if you can ask someone specific their opinion. But if "info@" is your only option, then send away, because modeling agencies try not to miss a single picture if they can help it. Sometimes agencies even have the "info@" e-mail address automatically forwarded into another person's e-mail, to protect privacy. Every agency wants to discover the next supermodel, *especially* if he or she is sitting right in their in-box!

One of the main problems with e-mail is that people get inundated by advertising or spam, and they delete the majority of their e-mails without looking at them first. Here are some tips on how to send an e-mail to catch someone's attention and not let that happen.

On the "subject" line of your e-mail type your first name only, height, age, and what division you are trying for, then in the body of the e-mail put your personal message and measurements (but keep it *very* short). If you are *not* e-mailing a specific person, and there are several divisions within the agency that you are contacting, you should put what division you are trying for in the body of the e-mail as well. Only send one e-mail per division! And never combine divisions; send separate e-mails to separate divisions—an agent doesn't want to see that you are marketing yourself to just any division; they want to feel special and that you sent your pictures to them alone. An example of a message for an e-mail to a high-fashion modeling agent would be:

Subject Line: Taylor, 5'10", age 17, high fashion

Dear Nicole,
My name is Taylor, and I am from Portland, Oregon.

> Height: 5'10"
> Bust: 34
> Waist: 24
> Hips: 35
> Eyes: Blue
> Hair: Brown

Please reply to this e-mail if you are interested in representing me in your high-fashion division.
If you are not interested, I would be grateful for some advice as to another agency I could contact.
Thank you,
Taylor Smith

Short and sweet! If you write too much, it won't get read. In the subject line you can abbreviate if you have to, for "high fashion" put "high fash." and for "commercial print" put "comm. print," and so on. And don't expect a reply, but once in a while someone will answer if you keep trying, *especially* if you are specific and to the point.

If you are a male model, just replace the bust and hips measurements with your suit size, and keep in the waist measurement.

Only send three pictures: two head shots (one smiling, one not smiling), and a full-length frontal body shot in a bathing suit. *For the high-fashion divisions, arrange the nonsmiling head shot in your attachment so that it is opened first; use a smiling head shot on top for the others.* Be careful, sometimes if there are too many pictures attached, the e-mail will not open. This has happened to me as a manager many times. Or if the re-cipient sees too big of a file, they may delete it and not even open it. Three pictures by e-mail is *perfectly* acceptable! If they are interested (and an agent *will* be able to tell from the pictures I taught you to take), then they will ask for more photos by mail, or request that you come in and meet them. *To leave them wanting more is a better way to catch their attention than sending too many photos and making it appear as if you are desperate.*

Make sure you request a return receipt so you know if it got there. Again, getting a specific name and e-mail address is always the best way. But if you are not able to, send your pictures to the general e-mail address anyway. It just may take longer to get a response, and if you get a return receipt request but no response, at least you know that your pictures have been received by *someone*.

PRESENTATION

Okay, ladies and gentlemen . . . you are now ready to strut your stuff! You have already figured out by this point what category of modeling suits you best, where the agencies are in the world that you are target marketing for your mailings, have key phrases memorized, such as "commercial look" or "test," and practiced taking digital pictures many, many times with a friend or family member, right?

This next section, about presentation, will help you when you start getting request appointments from the pictures you send to agencies, or if you have modeling agency open calls accessible to you. "Presentation" is all about castings, open calls, callbacks, what they are, how to find them, what to bring, what to wear, how to *present* yourself in front of an agent, and what to say. And you thought this business was easy! It only *looks* easy.

The Difference Between Castings and Open Calls

A "casting" is a call for an audition from a client for a specific kind of model. After you sign on with an agency, you will be going on a lot of castings to try out for jobs. Castings are just like auditioning or interviewing; you go and meet the client and try to be the one that is selected, or at least get a callback for the next round of castings. In the case of a casting, the client will narrow down sizes, hair color, age, etc., as opposed to an open call, which is more of a general request. A good example is when Bloomingdale's catalog calls an agency looking for blond girls who are five eight to five ten, ages twenty to twenty-six. Bloomingdale's is narrowing down the model pool by picking specific attributes they would like to see in order to fulfill their need for a particular catalog or advertisement that needs to be shot. A *request* casting is when Bloomingdale's calls and specifically requests your name to invite you to their casting because they have a specific interest in you beforehand, which is usually the result of your agency marketing you to the client. Sometimes request castings are only you and the client, privately held in his or her office.

An "open call" is usually held for a more general request for models, with many more people attending as opposed to when a casting is held. Agencies looking for new faces will hold "open calls" on a particular day, usually once a week. If Bloomingdale's held an open call, they would just call the agency and tell them to send them every model they have that would be appropriate for their catalog, without narrowing down the specifications.

Sometimes you will see open call casting ads in the newspaper, which you need to be very careful about. These ads make it sound as if modeling jobs are waiting for you if you just sign up, when in reality, they are people trying to take your money once you get into their offices, or to the hotel or place where they are hosting the "open call." In New York City, modeling agencies are not allowed to publicly advertise—but model searches are different. Managers and scouts may have open calls, searching for new talent, though when they do, be sure to ask all of the questions I list for you toward the end of chapter 6, under "If You Are Approached by Someone Who Says You Should Be a Model."

How to Find Open Calls

In New York City, all of the larger agencies (Next, Ford, IMG, Elite, and Wilhelmina, to name a few) have lists of at least eight to ten of the best agencies in New York with times and days of their open calls. They are held every week. The way to find this list is to go to one of those agencies and ask the receptionist for a copy of that list. You can try calling the receptionist of one of the modeling agencies and have them fax it to you, if you can find someone nice enough to take the time, or on the Internet there is information available on some agencies' Web sites about open calls. Models.com is a very informative Web site, with a lot of the more popular agencies' names. Take the names, Google them, and find their Web sites, because if they have an open call it is usually on the site toward the back. Always call to confirm the times and location, because agencies sometimes move locations or change or cancel open calls on a particularly busy week, like during fashion show season. I decided not to put a complete list of agencies in this book, because sometimes agencies go out of business or move, and you need to obtain an up-to-date list when you are ready to start going on open calls. It's easy enough—just follow the steps I've given you.

Start calling the lists of agencies in your area. Ask them if they host open calls, and when. Find out whom you are speaking to, and ask *them* if you can send them a picture! Most agents will say yes. Do you know why? Because they do not want to miss out on someone who may be a potential supermodel or financially successful model, or both. Can you imagine if someone became a superstar at one agency and told everyone that so-and-so at another agency was rude to him or her when they first started? No agent or manager wants to be the "one who turned so-and-so down." If the agent tells you that you do not need a name to attention your mailing to, then *politely* hang up the phone and just make sure to put what division you are targeting on the front of the envelope.

When you are calling to inquire about open calls, and you are a high-fashion potential candidate, it doesn't hurt to also ask for the new-faces division to try to get an appointment. This will be an easier task in the secondary markets. In the larger cities, they will insist on seeing photos first and then will proceed from there. That is a big reason why you need the correct photos *before you start calling agencies*. If someone requests your pictures, you should send them without wasting any time, because he or she will forget you before you know it.

Google the key words "modeling," "modeling agencies," "models," "model search," and you will find more information on your search for an agency. You may even find some legitimate modeling contests to enter while doing this! Just be careful about any Web sites that ask for your credit card or try to charge you. The majority of the Web sites that post modeling pictures do *not* have agents searching for models on their site anyway, and you will be better off making your own contacts. I get into more detail about Web site scams and how to spot them in chapter 6. If you find a model search when you start researching agencies, investigate it to make sure it is a reputable one. Some of them are free, and others charge a minimal processing fee.

Now, let's discuss how to present yourself once you've done the research to find the open calls.

What to Wear

Wear a *simple* outfit that is comfortable. Body-conscious outfits are best (clothes that show off your shape but are not skintight), and remember keep clothing *very simple!!!* Agents absolutely do not want to see your latest clubbing outfit. The more complicated and flashy your outfit gets, the more you will take the attention away from yourself, and that is a hindrance, not a benefit. Besides being glitzy or gaudy with too much jewelry, makeup, or by wearing loud colors, you can overdo it by looking too "sexy" as well. Low-cut V-necks, micro minis (unless you are really skinny), or skintight anything is a bit over the top. Think about trying to look naturally captivating and you won't overstate your presence when someone first looks at you. Remember, agents can be intimidated too!

GIRLS (AND LADIES)

Tank tops are great for showing off arms, shoulders, and neck. There are multitudes of tank top choices out there these days, even if you are not in your teens. Just be realistic—if you are around thirty-five years old or older, skip over the wife-beater tank tops and wear a type of tank that is more age appropriate. Jeans are fine, as long as they fit you *perfectly*. You definitely want to keep your outfit on the casual side so it doesn't look like you are trying *too* hard, and ladies who are a bit older: if you dress junior you will look like you are trying *way* too hard! Dresses are okay, as long as they are simple, elegant, and not too revealing. One of the biggest turnoffs in this industry is a girl or woman walking into an agency with cleavage up to her chin or her breasts falling out of her shirt. You will get a chance to bare your body if the agency is interested in you, because they will ask you to change into a two-piece bathing suit for measurements and Polaroids. If you think your décolletage is your best asset, then show it in the bathing suit pictures I taught you to take, not at an appointment with an agency you are trying to impress for the first time.

Here are the rules for makeup application: *NO makeup* if you are going for the high-fashion category or for children. For every other category, *light makeup only:*

- Cover stick for covering pimples or circles under the eye
- Sheer powder for shine on the face
- Light mascara
- Sheer or neutral lip gloss
- Natural nails

Sound familiar? These are some of the same rules I taught you to follow when you take your pictures!

BOYS (AND MEN)

A simple T-shirt and jeans will work when you go to the agencies. Do not dress up too much; you do not want to look as if you are trying *too* hard, or appear to be nervous or stuffy. Tank tops are fine in warm weather, although if you're heading toward thirty-five years of age, you should probably keep it to short sleeves. Slacks and a polo shirt are nice for older gentlemen, as you will be trying to convey a more classic look, as opposed to a younger, trendy, or "skateboarder"-type look.

I discussed shaving before, in my tips for getting ready to take your nonprofessional pictures, and you should go with those same rules for seeing agencies in person. If you are not shaved in the pictures you sent in to a certain agency and they request to see you, then show up at your appointment unshaven. If you *did* shave and they request to see you, then go that way. Consistency is so important! If you are going on an open call and aren't sure, then reread the section in chapter 2 under "Appearance" and try to decide which option is best for you.

OTHER TIPS ON WHAT TO WEAR

One of the most important things to remember when going to see model agencies in person is that too much makeup and jewelry is an *instant* turnoff, *especially* if you are under twenty-five years of age. You should definitely moisturize though (and not with a self-tanner) if you are female, and men should do a few push-ups before walking into the office, especially if you have a buff body. It tightens the muscles to high-light them a bit, and brings color to your cheeks for a healthy glow.

Do not dye, cut, or style your hair differently from how you wear it every day, unless your everyday look is a punk rocker. Again, you will only look like you are trying too hard, and they will want to redo your look as soon as they sign you anyway—just as I described how they want the photos in your portfolio done their own way—and if you have potential, they will spot it *raw*. Wear your hair the way I described it in the "Appearance" section in chapter 2—clean and natural, and without radical colors or streaks of *any* color—even blond.

Ladies, do *not* wear high heels if you are not comfortable in them, or do not know how to walk confidently in them. And do not wear high heels with a *micro* miniskirt, which is another instant turnoff when walking into an agency for the first time—trust me! Regular miniskirts are fine, especially if you have great legs, but do not pair a mini with a top that is too revealing or too tight—it will just make you look like you are trying too hard. The key is to pull off a casual, yet put-together look that you feel comfortable in, but that also shows off your body at the same time. Got it? Good!

What to Bring

Bring the pictures with you that I taught you to take of yourself, as they are not done by a professional photographer, and these are the ones agents prefer to see. Color laser copy these pictures at Kinkos, or another office supply store, so you will have copies for each agency. Just make sure the pictures are very clear—no blurry spots, blemishes, or funky colors in them.

Arrange them in the same way that I told you to in chapter 2, with your name, height, age, measurements, clothing size, hair color, eye color, city where you are from and *phone number (most important!)* on the back of each one. Bringing these pictures is just to reassure yourself that the agency will have something to look at when you leave if they do not take pictures of you themselves. Then you are prepared to leave them with pictures similar to the ones they would have taken anyway. It *is* nice to have a backup plan just in case the agency camera is broken or they suddenly run out of film—don't laugh, it's happened to me as a modeling agent!

As I said, if an agency likes you, most likely they will take Polaroids or digitals of you anyway, and *voilà*! You will already be wearing the proper clothing, you will have your makeup done (or not done, if you're younger or a potential male model), and will already know how to pose for the camera. Sometimes when an agency takes pictures, that is the deciding factor on whether or not they are going to take you on as a model. It is easy to tell if someone is a natural in front of the camera as soon as he or she starts having their pictures taken. By following my advice and with *lots of practice*, you will already know the best angles of your face, the different expressions you are able to make, etc., and will be more confident and natural in front of a camera that someone you don't know is holding.

REMINDER . . .

If an agency does not already represent you, then any professional pictures you have will most likely *not* be used when you start in that market, especially in the larger markets like New York. *Even if you have an agency*, most of the time the pictures you took in that market will not apply to a different market. Just like the specific Polaroids or digital pictures that the agencies like for their picture submissions, modeling agents want to put together your portfolio *their* way, with their own photographers taking the pictures. This is true not only for a model who does not have representation but also for models who have agencies in other markets, especially if they are smaller markets. Most models still find that new professional pictures are necessary when they arrive in new markets. So when I tell you that you only need to bring nonprofessional pictures to open calls, please listen. It may even *hurt* your chances if you bring professional pictures you had done on your own!

How to Present Yourself

Only attend open calls or send pictures if you are looking and feeling your absolute best—if you are not looking your best, then wait until you are. First impressions always count! The modeling business will still be around by the time you are ready, and you will only be more confident and prepared and on your way to a solid career if you wait until you are completely ready.

Looking your best involves weight considerations, emotional preparedness, and outward appearance. I already prepped you in the beginning of this book about the importance of being and staying fit, and that emotionally you will need to make a personal commitment about whether to start a modeling career or not. Regarding your outward appearance, your face is probably the first thing people notice, especially in the modeling industry, and it needs attention, just like the rest of you. Skin care is an integral part of your outward appearance, and a skin-maintenance routine should be followed just as carefully as your fitness or nutrition plan. You should clean your face and apply moisturizer routinely, along with sunscreen, every day. When you go to see modeling agencies in person, your skin should be relatively clear, and if it isn't, wait until it is before you start scheduling appointments. As I told you about being in shape, it will not hurt you to wait a few months to present yourself in front of an agency, because the better the first impression you make, the better chance you have of getting representation.

By the time you have finished reading this book, you should have a good idea of what is involved in becoming a model and how to take the best pictures that you can on a physical as well as a mental level. It demands a bit of confidence, a heap of patience, and a large dose of determination. You have to be ready for all that and not let anyone steer you differently, or put a negative spin on any of your dreams. Just present yourself as a total package in the best way possible.

THE RIGHT ATTITUDE

Agents look for overall attitude as well as particular "looks"; you can't seem too desperate or nervous, or they will notice immediately. Try to cover any nerves with a nonchalant attitude, but still appear friendly and *confident*. Even overconfidence is better than desperation! But being arrogant is a turnoff, so don't cross that line. Take a few deep, slow breaths before walking into your meeting, as this really helps settle the nerves. *Time* magazine had an article in their January 29, 2007, issue on ways to beat stress, and the first one mentioned was breathing deeper and slower to *instantly* slow down your heart. It really works! Meditate, pray, stay away from caffeine the day you meet with an agency, or figure out whatever it takes for you to control those nerves *before* walking into an open call or appointment.

Perhaps if you try to imagine what is most likely going to happen when you walk into an open call, it will help you calm your nerves a little more. If you are one of those people who never get nervous, then read this anyway, in case your first attack of nerves strikes right when you see a modeling agent for the first time!

Picture this (no pun intended) . . . you walk into the lobby of whatever agency is hosting the open call, and there are other girls or guys waiting there in line (unless you are first), and a sign-in sheet with names on it. Someone will eventually call your name. You will then follow that person to a conference room or office where you will be interviewed. The person in that room (usually a booker from whatever division is hosting the open call, or a scout for the agency) decides who has potential for modeling with that agency and who doesn't, and he or she will look at you, ask you a few questions, and evaluate your pictures.

If you do not have pictures, it is okay to go on an open call without them. I just wanted you to have the ones I taught you to take as a backup, but if you are on an open call and an agency thinks you have potential, they don't *need* to see pictures of you; they will take photos of you themselves. So many people do not realize this very important fact—*having no pictures is so much better than having second-rate professional ones*. But if you have the ones I showed you how to take—even better.

Either way, if the person who is hosting the open call thinks you have potential they will take Polaroid or digital pictures of you to show to the other agents right then and there. If that happens, first thing you need to do is *relax* . . . if you are too nervous, the camera will detect it. You would be surprised at how the lens of a camera can look into your soul!

There is no need to "strike a pose," as you may think. The first picture will most likely be a straight-on frontal head shot, *just like the ones I taught you how to take.* As a matter of fact, you probably won't come across anyone who wants to represent you who takes any pictures other than those described in this book! That is why it is so important to practice, because you now have the tools you need to be ultraprepared, and it will come naturally to someone who has done it over and over. Whoever is going to take the picture will show you where to stand, whether it is against a wall, or outside, or someplace else. You can even ask the person taking the pictures if they want you to smile or not, have your hair up or down, etc. It is *perfectly* okay to ask questions! The person taking the pictures may even tell you something in their answer that you may not have thought of or had forgotten—because of nerves—about the instructions in this book on how to take a Polaroid or digital picture.

You will have to turn on the attitude that you want to show in those pictures *instantly,* and you won't have time to fix your hair or change your clothes, you need to be camera-ready at any moment. That's why I told you how to dress and look when you walk into an open call, so you will be ready to go! Sound stressful? It is all part of being a model. If you are a model you are being watched and photographed *all* the time. You will have to instantly switch from nonchalant, friendly banter, sitting at a conference table with an agent, to immediately standing up and imagining you are on a photo shoot for *Vogue* magazine in Italy—only with a Polaroid camera and a harried booker. Get used to it! This will hopefully be your new career, and that's what modeling is all about.

WALKING THE WALK

First of all, you will not have to "walk" for an agency if you are not in the realm of high fashion. This is a quite common misunderstanding that is encouraged by modeling schools and conventions because one of the things they take your money for is teaching people how to "walk"— no matter what age, size, or shape you may be. And if you *are* trying out for high fashion and you do not know how to walk, and if an agency thinks you have a look that will work well for the runway, one of the bookers will teach you how to walk, or that agency will hire a trainer for you. No lessons are needed before joining an agency! They will mold you appropriately.

With all that said, if you are a high-fashion candidate and would like to be prepared if an agency does ask you to "walk," the most important thing you should remember is to do it *naturally.* The next few tips for walking should be done in a casual way; don't exaggerate anything to the point where it seems awkward.

- Before you start walking, gather yourself together at the beginning of whatever runway you are given, throw your shoulders back, put your head slightly higher than eye level, keep your eyes straight ahead, and pull your torso up and in to make yourself look taller. Then strike the bathing suit pose that I told you to use when taking your pictures, the one where one leg is bent elegantly, with the ball of your foot delicately balancing the bent leg.

■ With your posture now set, take long strides across the floor, placing one foot in front of the other, as if you were walking on a balance beam, with a confident look on your face. Keep your strides natural and slow—in other words, don't start swinging your shoulders or moving your hips more than you do when you walk naturally. The slower the better, because people tend to walk faster when they are nervous.

■ Make sure that your arms are only *gently* swinging as you walk, because a lot of arm movement looks clumsy. To create a more flowing look, try to keep your shoulders still while you are walking. *Glide* across the floor as if you were floating and you have control of every movement you make.

■ Fancy turns? These are for the professionals! Leave this type of thing to Naomi Campbell until you get with an agency and learn it the right way. Walking down the runway isn't as showy as it used to be anyway. Designers prefer a smooth, more elegant gait with less posturing, so just try to be natural, and don't try anything too dramatic, just a simple stop and played-down turn at the end of your mock runway is fine. It's all about the attitude you are carrying while you walk the walk and the sense of star power that radiates from your body language toward your audience.

Now, just because I tell you to keep it natural and simple, don't think so much about how your body is moving that you forget that there has to be confidence displayed in your face. If you look bored, whoever is watching you will probably be bored as well. Imagine you are on a huge runway in Paris in front of dozens of magazine editors and famous photographers, being paid $20,000 to walk in a show, a gorgeous evening gown clinging to your body in all the right places as you walk on five-inch stilettos, or if you are a man, a beautiful hand-made custom tuxedo that fits you perfectly, with sneakers made to look like dress shoes. Know deep inside that you are the hottest model alive, with the most to offer. And in your mind make sure you are thinking, If this agency doesn't want me, it is *their* loss."

Once again, this all comes more naturally with practice! But if you forget everything else, make sure you are at least standing up straight with your shoulders back, head up, and looking confident when you walk for someone. And yes, you will have to do all of this in a small conference room, or perhaps in the lobby with people watching, so be prepared to do exactly that, and transport yourself to Paris in your mind as soon as you take the first step.

What to Say to a Modeling Agent

So . . . you finally got in to see someone who works at an agency in person. Now what do you do? You know what to wear, what to bring, and how to act, but what do you *say*? Yes, models have to speak on some occasions. I told you before that the best way to enter into this business is to be your own manager. Well, that manager (you) is going to have to step up to the plate and sell *you*. You need to try and pull all the information you can out of each person that you meet without going overboard. ASK QUESTIONS!!! Do not leave without an answer, but *do not take any of those answers personally* either, just learn from them. Knowing the right questions can be the key to mapping out a plan to reach your specific goals! Asking the right questions will show more of your personality and perhaps will make you less nervous by keeping you fully engaged in the conversation.

Here are some questions to ask if you got turned down by an agency; pick one or two that you think would help you move forward, and if the agent gives you more time, keep asking more questions! Write down the answers, because when you get home and don't remember what they said, you will have a hard time trying to track that person down to tell you again. As a matter of fact, if you try to do that, it will only annoy the person who took the time to give you advice in the first place.

QUESTIONS TO ASK IF AN AGENCY
DOES *NOT* WANT YOU

1. **WHAT CAN I DO DIFFERENTLY AT THE NEXT OPEN CALL (OR CALLBACK) I ATTEND?** This is quite a broad question, but if there is one glaring error that you made with your hair, makeup, clothing, pictures, or anything else, this gives the agent a chance to let you know what he or she thinks about the first impression you made.

2. **AM I SEEING THE RIGHT DIVISION?** This is a good question to ask because it is not normally information someone working at an agency would volunteer. Open calls tend to move quickly, and if it is a high-fashion agency, then the focus will be on high fashion. If you mention to the person who is running the open call that you are open to other divisions, then perhaps they will suggest something different for you, or give you some advice, such as to move on to a different agency or category.

3. **WILL YOU SEE ME AGAIN IF I GAIN EXPERIENCE?** In other words, do they think you could start in a smaller market and work up to the kind of experience that they are looking for? Or maybe the agent thinks it would be a good idea if you tried to get into a European agency first to get some tear sheets? If you are marketing yourself in a competitive market such as New York City, this may be the case. This is a question I always used to ask agents as a model if I was rejected, because some agencies are not big into developing models from the beginning, but will consider taking you on at a future time when you have more experience. Remember? That's how I finally got into Ford Models in New York. I was too old for the "development" division, but too young for the main board, so I went to Europe, gained experience and tear sheets, and was ready to start working with a solid portfolio in the high-fashion main division when I got back to the United States. The same thing could happen to you!

4. **DO I NEED TO LOSE WEIGHT OR EXERCISE?** Brace yourself—you will most likely get the truth. If the answer to this is no, then it *is* mostly likely the truth. An agent or manager will not volunteer information about your weight unless they are thinking about taking you on as one of their models. For example, someone may say to you, "We would like to sign you, but you need to lose ten pounds first. When you have lost the weight come back and see us, and we will start sending you to see clients." But if they don't volunteer any comments about your weight and you *ask*—now that is a different story. Then you need to make sure you are ready for the answer to be yes, because an agent will say exactly what he or she thinks and you need to be prepared for that. Take this advice seriously, but not personally. Think about what the agent said and that the answer of yes to the question whether you need to lose weight could be taken two ways—it could be that you need to buckle down and start working out, or it could simply mean that you are targeting the wrong division.

First ask where the problem is. Most of the time there is a target area that you may need to trim down or tone up, and it is something you can fix with a healthier diet and exercise. If an agent says you need to lose weight all over, then you did not follow my process correctly. Something is amiss between the requirements I gave you, and the measurements that you think you are. Be careful of this—you need to figure out what happened by going back and comparing your measurements with the category descriptions. Once again, ladies and gentlemen, be honest about your measurements or this whole process I am teaching you will not work to your most ultimate benefit, and the advice I give you will not mesh with the responses you get from agencies.

5. **SHOULD I CUT MY HAIR OR CHANGE MY APPEARANCE IN ANY WAY?** Listen to what a modeling agent has to say about this! Don't make the same mistake I did with my hair, when I refused to cut it at the request of several agents and

hairstylists. But at the same time, don't go cutting off your hair after only one person tells you to do so. Have you ever heard of the phrase "one man's trash is another man's treasure"? Well, your hair could mean two different things to two different agencies, so you need to do thorough research before you do anything that is drastically different. Ask several different industry professionals, including agents, hairstylists, and photographers for their opinions. Especially for men, the difference between a long-haired surfer-boy look and a crew-cut, preppy-male look is huge and should be dealt with carefully. Infinite patience is required in this business, and should be utilized when changing *anything* about your look.

6. **DO YOU KNOW OF ANY OTHER AGENCIES THAT MIGHT LIKE MY LOOK?** Most of the agents have friends at other agencies who will see models by appointment. A lot of agents have worked at other agencies as well and usually know offhand which agency is looking for what kind of specific model. If you can get someone to refer you, this is a *major* bonus. Either the person referring you will call and make an appointment for you, or you may have to call yourself and use the person's name to get an appointment. Treat the referral with respect, and if you get an appointment, do not call them before the assigned time when they will be seeing you, unless you can't make it or are running late. Even then, you should speak with the receptionist, so as not to bother the agent, and let the receptionist know you are running late for your appointment with that booker. Try not to be late though—it creates a negative first impression before the agency even knows what you look like.

Try to get specific contact names within an agency if you can and write down their suggestions, being extra careful that you write down everything correctly. Getting specific names of people working in agencies is a vital part of breaking into the business, because you can then get personal direction for the type of modeling you are appropriate for, or advice on how, being the particular type you are, you can move forward in the business. Every person you can see or speak to that you are referred to brings you a step closer to getting where you want to be. As I said before, anyone can tell you, in general, to "send in pictures," but it's getting to the right people for your type of look that will get you the furthest in the long run.

If you *are* given a contact name to send your pictures to or call, do *not* dally! Send your pictures immediately to that person, the same day, if possible. The reasons for this are because agents move around constantly, to different divisions or sometimes totally different agencies, and if you have a contact name, you want to catch them while they are still there, and not at a different agency, or perhaps out of town. Also if the person that gave you the contact name of an agent (or manager) spoke to him or her about you, you are still fresh in their minds if you send your pictures right away or call, whatever the case may be.

QUESTIONS TO ASK IF AN AGENCY *WANTS* YOU TO JOIN THEM

1. DO I HAVE TO SIGN A CONTRACT? Signing a contract depends on the agency. Smaller markets don't emphasize contractual agreements as strictly as some of the bigger markets do, but it all depends. If you have done your research and have found a strong, reputable agency, then do not hesitate to get into a contractual agreement. But always read everything you sign and understand it thoroughly. Get a lawyer to look it over if possible, and if you are under eighteen, you will need to have a parent or guardian sign it for you.

2. IS THE CONTRACT EXCLUSIVE OR NONEXCLUSIVE? This is important, because if you sign an exclusive agreement, you are committed to that agency *and that agency only* for a certain period of time, in a chosen geographical area, which could be the entire United States, if the agency is a nationwide network. This may be favorable to you, or it may

not, depending on how well the agency is doing in the other states, or if you intend to travel within the United States to other markets.

Exclusivity is usually offered only in the bigger markets, but if you sign an exclusive contract in a smaller market, be aware of the conditions of the contract. For example, in smaller markets usually the contract will only include a regional area, and if it doesn't, it can be negotiated. This means that the chosen agency does not expect to place you in another market and get a commission. They are only concerned about getting you work in their part of the country. This is not a bad way to start, you will gain experience from this agency and market, yet will still be free to do what you want in a bigger city where it is of great benefit not to be exclusively signed to any agency while you are searching for representation.

3. WHAT IS YOUR COMMISSION STRUCTURE? The standard commission that is taken out from print jobs is 20 percent. (Commercial print is sometimes 10 percent, depending on the type of agency that booked the job, for instance talent agencies that book print work usually take only 10 percent from the model. But high-fashion agencies take a 20 percent commission.) If your agency is being paid the standard commission, for example, and your day rate for a particular job is $2,000, then you will net $1,600 from the agency, depending on your debt with them, of course. Most agencies are negotiable on the commission percentage after a model starts making upward of $250,000, but that is between you and the agency. Also, your net pay unfortunately does not include taxes being deducted, just to let you know. Taxes are a separate issue, and I delve more into how that works in chapter 7.

4. ARE YOU A LICENSED AGENCY? Check out the laws to find out whether or not a modeling agency needs to be licensed at the local Department of Consumer Affairs or state attorney general's office. If an agency does not have a license and the government requires one for that area, be careful, they may be scam artists. Most of the larger states require

"employment agency" licenses for the modeling agencies. You can check with the Department of Consumer Affairs for license verification. Managers are different, because they do not directly book work for the models. I also tell you in chapter 7 how you can research agencies in more detail.

5. **WILL YOU ADVANCE MONEY FOR THE JOBS I BOOK, OR DO YOU WAIT UNTIL THE CLIENT PAYS?** Some agencies will advance you money on the work you perform. If an agency doesn't advance money, and they give the client up to 60 days to pay, then you will have to wait until the agency gets paid before you get your money. Some clients take 90 to 120 days to pay—it all depends. Other agencies will advance a small portion of your money, and then the rest when the client pays. Find out what the agency's payment plan entails, and see if they are willing to negotiate a plan that is advantageous to you.

6. **DO YOU REQUIRE A CERTAIN AMOUNT OF MONEY TO BE SPENT IN CREATING A PORTFOLIO?** Some modeling agencies will make money by selling photo packages up front—you have to give them the money before you see the pictures or join their agency—and this is *NOT the way to do business, besides it is illegal in some states!* It is also unethical if the agency you are with asks for cash from you before you see any pictures. I've already explained to you about not needing professional pictures before you get into an agency, but after you are with an agency there is a right way and a wrong way to do business as far as photo shoots are concerned. Reputable agencies in the high-fashion category will set you up with photographers who charge only for expenses, or who are free because the photographer is trying to establish himself/herself as well, but for everyone else who has to pay (and high-fashion models sometimes have to pay for more than expenses to test), be careful about how you and your transaction with the photographer or agency are being handled.

In addition, the agency will often advance you money for pictures until you start working. If not, make sure you get a receipt from the photographer and are not charged more than $150 per shoot (for high-fashion models), plus extra fees if there is hair, makeup, and/or styling being done. The average price of a test with hair, makeup, and styling for high fashion is from $300 to $500, but these photographers (who work with reputable agencies) have already proven themselves talented enough to charge those rates. If you are in a division other than high fashion, expect to pay $500 to $600 per shoot. Sorry to the people who are not in high fashion, but that is just the way the business operates. A bit of advice: do *not* pay a photographer until you have seen the pictures, because if you need to reshoot, there is no motivation for the photographer to reschedule if they already have their money.

So basically this is a trick question, because there should be *no* preestablished requirement on how much money you need to spend to make a portfolio. One or two photo shoots are set up to get your initial pictures, and then you and your agent decide if you are getting the pictures you need as your career moves forward and you test more, or you start working. Comments from clients and/or jobs that you get will all have a say in your need for more pictures down the road. So if someone tells you that you need to spend a certain amount of money in creating a portfolio to start modeling, please be cautious. It's a fine line—models can work at their own pace making their portfolio, but they still need pictures in order to work. If you feel you are being pressured about something though, ask questions, and find out what the real deal is.

7. HOW MANY MODELS DO YOU REPRESENT, IN TOWN AND OUT OF TOWN? "In town" and "out of town" models are terms used to describe models who are either available for work locally or who are currently living in another market. Every agency has models who are either "in town" or "out of town." You will find out that a lot more models are "in town" in the agency's local area when the agency is located in a smaller city or town. In the larger modeling markets, a modeling agency will have a wall in their office with

composites displayed of models that are in town, and another wall in a separate location on which the models are all out of town. The reason *you* need to know about how many models there are in an agency is because it is a good gauge as to how big or small an agency actually is. Usually the answer to this question is not only a number but also an insight into the inner workings of a particular agency. You see, an agency should have explanations as to where most of their models are (if they are out of town), where they were placed, and what other agencies they are affiliated with in each country (a good way to get referrals, people!). So you will learn how well the bookers know their models, and what other agencies that particular agency works with around the world. This insight is key in getting to know an agency, as well as observing how knowledgeable they are about their models and other agencies around the world.

8. **HOW MANY BOOKERS DO YOU HAVE WORKING IN THE AGENCY?** There should not be more than fifteen or twenty girls in town for every booker in an agency in a *larger market*; if there are, you will not get individual attention. You and your assigned booker will develop a close, intimate working relationship as time passes. Modeling is an emotional career—if something is wrong in your personal life, it will show on the expression on your face in the pictures you take. Your booker has to be aware of mostly everything you are going through in your everyday life, be it a breakup of a personal relationship, an acne phase, or weight issues. Individual attention counts, especially when you need a helping hand in a foreign city or country.

Keep Marketing

If you do not have access to a larger city where you can go and visit agencies in person, continue to send your pictures in by mail as described in chapter 3. This is marketing—pure and simple. If an agency really wants you, you'll never know how it can be worked out to your advantage to sign with them unless you try. Don't let limitations of geography stop you from marketing yourself around the world. Most agencies have a budget to pay for plane tickets, hotel, etc., if they are genuinely interested in representing you and think you can make money in their market. Of course, you need to remember that these expenses are "advances," which eventually you'll need to pay back. They are deducted from your future earnings, sometimes with interest charges applied. There is more about advances under "Terms You Should Know" in chapter 7.

Even if an agency *does* want you, and you start a relationship with them, please keep in mind that it usually takes a significant amount of time to get work as a model, then more time after that to make an actual profit, *especially* on a regular basis. So you will need to make a bit of an investment on your part if the agency will not advance you money at first. Even after you have a portfolio and are ready to go on castings for work, sometimes it takes a while to get the hang of how to go on castings and impress the clients most, or of how to take pictures that are appropriate for your type of look using the suggested photographers from the agency. Don't forget what I said about rejection as well! *Most* of the castings for jobs you get will not get you immediate work. Meanwhile, you can spend a significant amount of money trying to get a modeling career launched. The amount of your investment is up to you, and the agency can help you figure out along the way what direction to go—that is, whether you need to spend more money or just keep going on appointments, change markets, or whatever the case may be. In the meantime, get a part-time job, or something that brings in a little extra cash—I did! I was a hostess for a restaurant in New York City at night when I first started so I could still go on castings during the day, and when I lived in Miami Beach, I worked at the front desk of a hotel at night. Sometimes it takes a little juggling, but if you hang in there it is worth it in the end.

Callbacks

If someone has called you in from your mailings for an appointment to meet them or has called you back to their office again after an open call, this is a called a "callback." *Good for you!* What do you do now? No panicking allowed!

First, you need to make sure you have your pictures together in a neat and orderly fashion, just as I taught you how to do for the mailings, and make sure they are with you when you go on a callback appointment. It doesn't matter if the person you are meeting says they still have your pictures. If they get lost or misplaced, then you will still have something to give them to remember you by. You are better off safe than sorry, and it just gives the appearance of professionalism, which is always impressive.

I will now give you an idea (more or less) of what happens on a callback appointment, so you can be more prepared. When you arrive at the agency, most likely there will be a receptionist, and he or she will summon the person who is requesting to see you, so make sure you have the first and last name of the person you are there to see. (At the larger agencies, if you do not have the name of the agent you are meeting, the person at the front desk will sometimes turn you away.)

You will probably be made to wait in the agency's lobby, reception area, or conference room for a few minutes after checking in until someone comes to meet you. The appointment will be only for you, so you can take your time to get to know the agency a little better than if there are a bunch of models all clamoring to see the same person in one day, like at an open call.

While you are waiting—I have never known a manager or agent to drop what they are doing and run quickly to their appointment with a new model, but you never know, I suppose—take some slow deep breaths in through your nose, and out through your mouth. Take a couple of breaths with your eyes closed and try to disappear for a moment and not think about where you are. Even if you are not nervous, this will give you a deeper sense of focus for meeting with someone who may become very important to you and your financial future. Just one deep breath will begin to slow down your heart rate, so if you are too hurried to close your eyes and do all the rest, at least take one deep breath to prepare yourself for your meeting.

Now that you are breathing more calmly, think about the questions you want to ask. I gave you a list of questions to ask, depending on whether an agency does or does not want you. (See pages 134–41.) Bring that list with you, pick a couple of questions from both sections, and take notes, because our brains play funny tricks on us when we are nervous. Whatever the outcome of this appointment, whether it is new representation for you or rejection, you will probably get vital information out of these people from some of your questions that will help you move forward in your career. If you get rejected, you might as well learn something from it, right? If you have a specific appointment with someone, even if they decide that you are not the right look for their agency, most likely he or she will be more receptive to you asking a couple of questions, as opposed to the craziness of an open call, where there is a lot less time for an agent to spend with any individual model.

Don't forget to smile, show lots of personality, and even joke around with the agent or manager, if it comes naturally. People like to work with other people who are easygoing and fun, especially in this business. It gets so intense behind the firing lines of a modeling agency, with all of the agents constantly in one another's faces and on the phone every minute of the day. So every bit of warmth and an outgoing attitude from a model is noticed. But most of all . . . be yourself. Don't get too caught up in the perceptions of what you think modeling is. If you can be yourself, your appearance and talent for modeling will shine through in the end.

5

FOLLOW-UP AND
COMMERCIAL ACTING

Whether you get a positive or negative response from your mailings or open calls, there is a certain amount of follow-up that needs to be done. Remember, you are looking at this from a business perspective, and nothing can be left undone or inconclusive. You need to learn as much as you can for your *next* mailing, or your *next* open call. A big part of modeling is evaluating the feedback to see how you can improve, so following up on what people are saying about you—or what they aren't—is crucial to continue marketing yourself.

Following Up Through Feedback and Evaluation

When professional models are working or attending castings or go-sees (a "go-see" is when a model who has representation is told by their agency to "go and see" the clients for the first time—a more detailed explanation is in chapter 7 under "Terms You Should Know") their agents are always calling up the clients and asking "What did you think of Nicole when she came to your casting?" or "Would you use Danny again for future work?" That is when it's the *agency's* turn to evaluate feedback and try to improve your image. Well, you need to do the same thing for *yourself* before you get an agency! Let me tell you how to go about doing this just the way the modeling agents do with their clients.

Go over what the agency said the day you attended an open call, and think about what you need to do differently to market yourself more appropriately. For the mailings, make follow-up calls to the people you marked "attention" to. You can only do this if you had a specific agent's name on the envelope, not if you sent pictures to a division in general.

Please don't count on the person remembering your pictures just because you sent something to their "attention"; the purpose of having a specific name on the envelope is getting someone to *open* the envelope and pay more attention to what is inside. Be ready to remind them of who you are, if they say they do not remember. And if they try to hang up, *let them*, and call someone else for the time being. Don't give up! *Someone* will eventually help you, but as I said—do not push it, and respect the fact that they are doing you a favor. I do realize follow-up calls to agents or managers may be difficult. Agents (particularly those in New York), do not like to be bothered with doling out advice to people they do not know. But there is a certain way to do it that may just catch their attention—remember, they are human too! An agent's *job* is calling clients all day to find work for their models, so you have a chance at someone being sympathetic toward you, but only if you are direct with them and smart about what you say. Oh, and be quick, their time is very valuable. Apologize for bothering them, figure out if they have seen your pictures yet, and ask your most important question, and then get off the phone quickly. More than likely they will get irritated with small talk, because they are on the phone eight to ten hours a day, barraged with calls.

The times that agents are less busy in the office are pretty standard around the world. Around ten in the morning is a good time to call, before it starts getting too busy, and after everyone has finished his or her first coffee. Another good time to call is about three, before the mad rush at the end of the day. *Do not* call a modeling agency after four-thirty, or during Fashion Show Week at *any* hour—agents are too busy at those times! Even if you do get someone to talk to you at those times, odds are that he or she will not pay much attention to you. Go on www.fashioncalendar.net to find out when the major shows are in each country, and stay away from calling agencies a week before those dates and up to a full week after the last day of their show season.

BE PERSISTENT, BUT NOT ANNOYING

DO NOT harass agencies; you will not get anywhere doing this. Modeling agencies usually will not send your pictures back, but maybe by making a follow-up call and asking some advice, you will make a new contact, or new information will be revealed to you that will help you move forward. You can *try* to have your pictures sent back to you by including a self-addressed stamped envelope, but don't count on it. If you don't get any answers the first time, wait eight weeks, take new pictures, send them again, and start the whole process over again. Ask for a "return receipt request" from the post office, so you know someone received them, and if you still do not hear, try, try again. Sometimes it takes several times of going to open calls or mailing in pictures to the same agencies, before they decide they are interested. Remember what I said in the introduction of this book? I got rejected by Ford New York four different times (from open calls), until a different agency in the States sent me to Europe, and I came back to Ford for the fifth time in Miami, then Ford Miami helped to get me into Ford New York. Let me try and explain why this happens.

Trends come and go, and many are cyclical, meaning that a certain look or style of a past season will come back around and be "in" again eventually. If you feel that your look is not "in" at the moment, it could be soon, because at any point in time your look could suddenly be what every magazine and designer wants to have, whereas you were nonexistent to them the year before. This is typically more the case for younger models (male *and* female). For the rest of you, the reason someone wasn't interested in you could have been that the agent had a headache that day, or saw you in a bad light, or a number of reasons that could actually have absolutely *nothing* to do with you as a potential model! That is why you have to keep plugging away.

WHAT TO SAY ON THE PHONE

When and if you get someone on the phone whom you sent your pictures to, first establish that the person you are talking to knows who you are so there are no mistakes. Do this by telling them your name, height, age, and where you're from, and if they seem in the least bit interested, try to make an appointment to see them in person. If they do not remember who you are or do not recall seeing your pictures, ask if you can send them by another means—for instance, if you sent them originally by mail, then try to get their e-mail address and e-mail your pictures to them. Or if you are not from the local area, ask them if you can send *more* pictures and ask what types of pictures they would like to see, for example, more body shots, closer head shots, etc. If they do *not* think you are the right look for their agency, choose some questions to ask out of the following list; they are similar to those in "Questions to Ask If an Agency Does *Not* Want You" from chapter 4, the difference being that the previous questions are useful when someone is meeting with you face-to-face, as opposed to a phone call, where someone is looking only at your pictures, and you are trying to get their advice to help you move forward with your search. The next group of questions focuses on how and if you need to take better pictures to market yourself (depending on how an agent answers the questions), and are from a more introspective approach so you can also go over them by yourself if you feel the need to remarket yourself from a different angle. Again, remember to be quick, and do not ask more than one or two questions, because an agent's time is very valuable and the last thing you want to do is annoy someone.

1. SHOULD I TARGET DIFFERENT DIVISIONS WITHIN THAT AGENCY OR SELECT A DIFFERENT TYPE OF AGENCY? If you did not get a chance to ask this question in person, as I suggested in chapter 4, "What to Say to a Modeling Agent," but you get someone on the phone who has your pictures or who has met you previously, then ask the first part of

this question if the agent works for an agency that has alternate divisions. If not, then ask if another agency might be better suited for your type of look. The response to that question may lead to other resources, such as a contact name at another agency, or open call information. You never know until you ask!

If you feel like you need to change your target market, try going over the "Model Identification" section in chapter 1 again to see if it opens more choices up to you. Carefully scan the "Categories of Modeling" and see if there is another category that is applicable to you. Is there another one you can try while you are marketing yourself to the others? Are you willing to start in a less prestigious category and work your way up the ladder? Or perhaps you need to start making money right away. If so, then promotional modeling could be an additional way to market yourself.

2. **DO I HAVE A STRONG ENOUGH LOOK FOR HIGH FASHION?** If you are trying out for high fashion, the agencies like models with distinctive looks, even if a girl has classic features. If you feel your look isn't getting the attention it deserves, ask people what you can do to alter it. Some agencies like very edgy, unique looks in their models, and there is nothing you can do to make that happen if that is not your genre. Remember, first try other markets or categories before you take *one* person's opinion too seriously. This is a very subjective question, but one that may be able to give you some answers in the high-fashion area.

3. **DID I WEAR TOO MUCH MAKEUP IN THE PICTURES?** This question may sound silly, but if you are younger (below the age of twenty-five or so), it could squash your chances and hinder your first impression, especially if someone can't truly see what you look like underneath too much makeup. And if you are older than twenty-five, people will suspect you are hiding something. I can't stress it enough—agencies *want* to see you without any makeup! They have a trained eye to spot potential models RAW. Like a painter, agents

like to work with blank canvases. Can you imagine if you were an artist, and you went to paint your first masterpiece, and there was already someone else's paint on the paper? You would be confused and distracted, trying to figure out how to begin to imagine your piece of art on this canvas with all of the paint in the way. Makeup has the same effect if there is too much on your face or if it is not necessary. It is distracting when applied too heavily or applied in the wrong way, and it is confusing because an agent will be wondering why you have it on in the first place (are you trying to cover something up?), and this will prevent the agent from being able to creatively imagine what kind of model you could be. To become a model is a creative process! As for the older girls, I already told you in chapter 4 about how much makeup you can get away with. Please, no more than is absolutely necessary.

4. **IS MY SKIN TOO TAN?** Agents and clients never like a girl too tan, unless she is doing ads for tanning lotion! Au naturel is the best, or just a little color that doesn't look too overdone (no pun intended). Tanning not only brings out wrinkles but can also be dangerous for the skin. Everyone should be wearing sunscreen every day. Though tan people tend to generally be thought of as "sexier"-looking, or even "healthier"-looking, tanning is truly a no-no in the industry of modeling, especially high-fashion modeling. How many supermodels can you think of that are deeply tanned, or have tan skin year-round? Not many. The *Sports Illustrated* swimsuit models perhaps, but that is only for that particular shoot, unless the model has a career as a bathing suit model, or is under contract with a suntan lotion or similar product. Tanning too much is bad for your skin and bad for a modeling career. Period. No exceptions.

5. **SHOULD I TARGET A WHOLE DIFFERENT MARKET?** This is not really a question you can ask on the phone too easily, because the person being asked would really have to see you in person to give you advice about a question such as this.

But perhaps think about it yourself . . . are you not getting a positive response from agencies in one particular area? Do people keep telling you "You're too commercial (or too edgy) for our agency?" If you are getting the "too commercial" response, then send your pictures to a smaller market, or pick a broader category. High-fashion models are a small percentage of the population, and commercial print models are a larger percentage, because there is a broader range of age and size accepted. So go easy on yourself, and try for a less competitive market! Did you start marketing yourself in a highly competitive city such as New York as a high-fashion model, when you live in Chicago and could have gotten a decent start modeling there? Afterward, you can always make the move to New York City when you are more experienced.

If people are saying you are "too edgy," then you have to try larger markets where an edgier look is more accepted, or perhaps Europe. People with unique characteristics are sometimes referred to as being "edgy," which is a look that may not be accepted in more commercial markets. The typical all-American blond bathing suit beauty from California may not be as accepted in a city like Milan, Italy, where "edgier" looks tend to garner more attention, and vice versa. Of course, there are exceptions. I can't make a rule for every look and every market, but trying to figure out these things can help you adjust finding your way to a market better fit for you.

Starting your modeling career in a smaller market is fine! Sometimes it is the smarter move. Do not underestimate the experience and work you can get in a smaller market. Like any other business, in modeling there are steps you can take to improve yourself at every level. Although the media likes to tout supermodels who were "overnight sensations," 99.9 percent of the population have had to work extremely hard at breaking into the modeling industry, *even with* an agency! Beginning models need to go on appointments every day and sometimes do not make money for *months* at a time. The more experience you have, the better.

How About Acting?

If you started sending out pictures or have been going to open calls for commercial print agencies, you may have run into the world of acting. Commercial print and commercial acting go hand in hand—in fact, many talent agencies, which book actors, also have commercial print divisions. Stacy Rosen, our expert agent from Greer Lange Agency who gave you tips about the commercial print arena in chapter 1, stresses that you should be open to all types of media when getting involved in the modeling industry:

Acting and modeling go hand in hand, and I find that most talent who does one, also does the other, or are eventually considered for the other. So I strongly believe that the more the talent can do at an agency, the better. . . . If an actor comes in wanting to act, we often end up booking them for commercial print, and vice versa—if a model comes in only wanting print work, we'll have them read for a speaking part so we can book them on commercial or industrial work and have fewer limitations when a client is browsing our whole portfolio of talent. This type of versatility between acting and modeling is very beneficial when it comes to our agency as well as other general commercial agencies that you will find.

Commercial acting is a whole different ball game than the world of fashion and print work, but you can send the talent agencies the same pictures that I taught you to take and send to modeling agencies. You *never* know when you have a certain look a commercial agency may be wanting for their roster. The spectrum of commercial acting is wide open as far as age, size, looks, etc. If you are not getting bites yet from modeling agencies, try and send your pictures in to talent agencies that have a commercial acting division. Address the envelope to the attention of the "Commercial Division." Also find out if that talent agency has a beauty division. Some agencies have a separate division that specializes in "beauty bookings," meaning commercials for makeup, hair products, skin care, etc. There are several agencies in New York City that have these divisions. You just have to call up the talent agencies and ask the receptionist if they have that particular division. The larger the agency, the more divisions it will have. CESD Talent Agency in New York City is a great example of a huge "talent" agency that has several divisions for television, including a beauty division and commercial print.

Talent agencies also have what's called "legitimate" acting, where the agencies book actors for theater, television shows, and film. They normally look for résumés that include professional black-and-white eight-by-ten head shots, as opposed to the fashion world, where so many people are signed from the nonprofessional, simplistic pictures I described in chapter 2. But again, you never know what an acting agency is looking for at a particular time, so it's better to send in your pictures even if you don't have a head shot and résumé right now. Just make sure you send a separate set of photos to the commercial division in addition to the modeling division because the two divisions are totally separate in a talent agency and no one is going to walk over to the other division to give them your pictures.

The whole point of a career in the modeling industry is being seen and getting out there, and trying *everything* you can do to make a name for yourself. When I was a modeling agent, I had commercial agents call me up and suggest a model who may be right for my agency, and vice versa, so the more you get yourself out there, the better chance there is of you being discovered. Crossover and multimedia marketing are very widespread these days, so if you want to get into modeling as a career, don't restrict yourself to only a few options. That's why I have been encouraging you not to put geographical limits on yourself and not to consider only one category, but to open yourself up to *all* of the options you may not have thought of, including acting.

If you *are* going to send your pictures in to talent agencies, let me give you a few tips:

- Do not send your pictures for the commercial print division and the commercial acting division in the same envelope. These are two separate divisions in a talent agency, therefore you should send two separate mailings. The "acting" side of a talent agency will not necessarily sign on the same people who are in their print division, and vice versa. All divisions within *every* agency are completely separate and should be treated as such.

- When you send your pictures to a commercial acting division, you should also include a résumé. Putting together a résumé is easy—just write down *any* experience you have had onstage (including high school and college), your skills (for example, skateboarding, diving, dancing, juggling, etc.), special training (for example, classes in martial arts or ballet), and list them in résumé form on a sheet of paper with your full name, address, and phone number with area code at the top. (Simple résumé formats can be found on the Internet for free.)

- If you are sending pictures only to the commercial print division, make sure the talent agency *has* a commercial print division, because not all talent agencies book print work.

Acting agencies are normally more formal than modeling agencies and have full-time receptionists, so do not expect to get through to an agent if you call. (It can be easier to speak directly to an agent at a modeling agency because frequently modeling agencies will have their agents answer the phone.) Send in pictures, but do not expect to get them back. You can always e-mail by return receipt request or put in a self-addressed stamped envelope if you want to try to get your pictures back, but there is no guarantee. If you *do* get your pictures back in a self-addressed envelope, at least you know *someone* saw your pictures!

You need the same determination and perseverance to break into acting as you do with modeling. It's the same sort of process of trying to be seen by someone in the industry, getting out of your house and making contacts, and doing everything you can to try and make a name for yourself. How do you know you will not meet someone that could possibly help you? You *don't* know, that's why you should try every angle.

Jesse, a commercial agent at one of the leading television and film agencies in New York City, answers some questions about the television market.

Judy: Do commercial agencies ever take on people from pictures they randomly receive in the mail?

Jesse: Actually, yes! Just like modeling agencies, commercial agents are constantly looking for new faces.

Judy: Can people send in the photos I described in this book?

Jesse: You can send in the more natural pictures for the commercial print department, but if you are looking to focus more on commercials and television, you should get an eight-by-ten head shot and résumé together. It gives you more of an edge for catching the eye of someone at a talent agency. Modeling is a little more "free" in the way that an agent can spot someone without makeup or their hair done in an instant, even from family pictures, but if you want to get into acting, there is a bit more formality involved. As much as having the right look is still very important, feeling comfortable in front of the camera and having some acting ability play a huge role as well. But if you don't have a head shot and résumé, you should send in the pictures that you *do* have anyway. You never know when someone will spot your look and call you in for an interview.

Judy: Any advice for models trying to break into television acting besides sending in pictures?

Jesse: My best advice would be to get into an acting class or take a workshop. It's a serious commitment, especially if you're interested in getting into film and television. In terms of commercials, there are a lot of commercial classes out there that you can take to help you appear more natural and feel more comfortable in front of the camera before going on auditions.

I have only touched on the subjects of commercial and legitimate acting, and there are some fantastic books out there for breaking into commercial acting or learning more about legitimate acting if you think that is a route you want to take. The Web site www.backstage .com is also an amazing source for people who want to break into the acting business. It contains vital information that you need as a wannabe actor, plus casting notices from around the world, if you subscribe to the Web site for a nominal fee. Do yourself a huge favor and research the acting industry just as you are doing with the modeling industry. Also contact your local Screen Actors Guild office (a union for television and film actors) and see if they have any suggestions about classes or workshops that you could take in your area.

Back to Modeling

When you follow up on your mailings or are going over the comments from modeling agencies' open calls, make sure that you deal with rejection positively. Rejection is a *huge* part of the entertainment business, whether you are an actor, model, singer, or dancer. I know I keep telling you this, but it is going to happen so much that I want you to make sure and remember the things I've said about it. I could write another book all about the rejection side of the fashion industry. Being turned down is just part of the business. It really is! *Every* model (and actor, for that matter) has been rejected by *someone*. It's a process, and learning from it and moving on are the best things you can do. It gets easier over time, and you will feel less insecure the more often it happens. You should be able to get to the point where if someone doesn't like your look or doesn't book you, you will automatically figure out if there is anything you can learn from it, or whether you should just ignore it and move on. If you cannot learn to live with rejection, you will never succeed in this business. I read somewhere that Cindy Crawford was told she should remove her mole—the mole that became her signature beauty mark. Someone told Gisele that her nose was too big and she would never be a model, and I'm willing to bet that Kate Moss was told she was too short more than once.

Brushing off rejection and moving forward will only make you a stronger person in the long run. Some negative comments you can learn from, and some you cannot, but sorting that out is the key. For example, if someone says you need to lose weight, then perhaps you learned you should try a different category, unless you are comfortable losing weight and can approach it in a healthful manner. It's all up to you—take the comments, negativity, and rejection and learn, learn, learn!

Once you are in the business, you will be told that you are too fat, too skinny, too dark-skinned, too light-skinned, that your hair is too short, too long, too blond, too dark . . . and all that will be said about the same model! Just remember that when people in the modeling business criticize you, they are seeing you as a commodity for their company, and you should not take it personally.

IF MORE THAN ONE AGENCY WANTS YOU

First of all—*congratulations!!!*

Having even just *one* agency interested in you is a huge accomplishment, but having multiple people wanting to sign you is a great feat indeed, and you should be proud of yourself. Choose wisely, and allow me to give you some crucial advice on how to make a very important (and hopefully long-term) decision for yourself.

You need to gather all the data that I taught you to find out in chapter 4, under "What to Say to a Modeling Agent," and figure out which agencies have the best answers to these questions. Then go in again to meet with the final few you are really serious about and see how you feel about them *emotionally*. Meaning, do you feel comfortable and at home in the office itself? Are the people friendly to you? Do they seem really excited at the prospect of representing you? The answers to all these questions should be a resounding yes. You almost want to have the feeling of a home away from home, because you will be spending a lot of time with them, and they will get to know you intimately. You will be speaking to them at least once a day, and if you are from out of town, they will be supporting you emotionally and possibly financially as well. A model once told me that you should feel as comfortable with your booker as you do with your own mother—that they are going to take the place of your mother and probably your therapist and best friend as well, as long as you are modeling with that agency. This is the case *especially* if you are younger, and even more so if you are in a foreign country. The job of an agent goes well beyond just getting a model work; if they are dedicated to their job, then they are there for you in every way imaginable. There must be a *passion* felt from that person (your agent) about your career.

Most of the agencies in a select market get relatively the same clients calling them for business, so you need to feel extremely comfortable with the personalities of the staff in the entire office, including all of the bookers, the director, and the owner. They should seem excited about you, be organized in a businesslike manner, and be confident that you will work in that market, or at least confident that they can place you in a market that will get you work eventually.

The agency you choose should have a marketing plan for selling you to clients. That plan could include sending you to Europe right away, keeping you in a local market to test and see clients for experience, or simply letting you know what type of clients they have in mind for you. For example, if an agency sees you as an editorial model, then they may want you to test with photographers right away, and ship you off to Europe for a couple of months. If you are not in New York, your agency may want to get you an agency in New York so *they* can groom you for Europe. If you have a more commercial look, your agency may want you to stay in their market so that both of you can make money. If that is the case, they should be able to tell you which clients work with the agency regularly, and to whom they are intending to market you, such as catalog clients (they should supply the names of catalogs they work with), advertising clients (they should supply the names of ad agencies or brand names they work with), and magazine clients they think your look would be appropriate for, if not the major editorial ones.

CONSIDER EVERYTHING, INCLUDING SMALLER AGENCIES

Sometimes models make the mistake of choosing an agency that has a famous name or is considered to be a high-profile agency just because of those reasons, without considering the kinds of people who make up the smaller agencies. If someone is really excited and passionate about representing you, but they are at a smaller, not as well known agency, you should definitely think long and hard about which agency to choose. Every agency has its advantages and disadvantages, but the relationship with the *booker* usually wins out in the end. When I worked as an agent at larger modeling agencies, sometimes the client would ask me to choose my "top five" favorite models, or tell me not to send *everyone* to a casting, but only a half dozen models who I thought were really appropriate for the job. Well, modeling agents are only human and will suggest the models they have a personal interest in first. As much as agents try to please the client or try to be impartial, they will first send their favorite models, or the ones they are friends with. It's only human nature! Also, some agents at the smaller agencies have worked for years at a larger agency and brought all of the better clients with them to the smaller agency.

The larger agencies have their advantages as well: longevity, financial stability, and a huge client database. So, what I am trying to say is that, when choosing an agency find out all you can about them, as well as where the bookers have worked before, how long they have been around in the business, and *always* keep in mind who seems to be the most excited and interested in representing you.

When an agency decides that they want you, then suddenly *you* have the upper hand! The ball is in your court now, and all of a sudden you go from trying to get an agency interested in you, to *them* wanting *you*! It's a feeling of exhilaration and triumph, but you must keep your feet on the ground and make sure that it is a decision that is right for you. You want a company that is legitimate as well as concerned about how *they* can work for *you*—not about how much money they can get out of you before you even start with them, which (as you have heard before) is a scam, and is covered in detail in chapter 6.

Your Future as a Model

Modeling can be full of glamour, fame, and fortune, where one has the potential to make several thousands of dollars in just a few hours, but it can also be challenging as well. But I'm going to be as honest as I can with you: modeling is not an easy business. It is a very demanding career and takes plenty of hard work, physically *and* mentally.

The first thing that a new model has to go through is repeated test-ing with photographers. Models have to test with an endless number of photographers to obtain the pictures they need to sell themselves. A test photo shoot can take anywhere from three to ten hours, depending on the photographer, and where the shoot takes place. Hair and makeup can take several hours alone! And all of this work is for no pay at all. Not many people will work for free, but models are *required* to all the time. Testing with photographers gives models experience as well as pictures for their portfolio—it is a sort of mock-up for the "real" jobs you will be doing in the future.

Appointments for jobs (which are called castings and go-sees—for their definitions see "Terms You Should Know" in chapter 7) are not scheduled every day. Meaning, there is sometimes a lot of downtime in between your jobs or appointments. You may get one appointment one day, seven the next, and none on the day after that, or for the next few days. When you first start a new market, there will probably be a lot of castings and go-sees the first few weeks or so, and then it slows down a bit. This is because the agency will send you around to see certain clients to introduce you to them in the beginning (go-sees), then you have to wait until someone is interested in you, or until some of the castings you go to turn into jobs. After the initial introduction in a market, your agency will hopefully have more cast-ings for jobs than go-sees, but sometimes models go for *weeks* with-out one single appointment! There are several reasons for this, and one of them is that the industry goes in waves, and you may be on the downswing of work opportunities at that point in time. Another rea-son may be that you have a unique look that is appropriate only for very specific jobs, and there just isn't enough work to keep you busy all of the time, or perhaps you simply just don't work very well in that particular market. Your agency will be able to let you know what the case is, and if you have to get new pictures, move locations, or anything else. They should be able to give you a straight answer about your future as a model in that market.

So even if you *do* sign with an agency, it doesn't necessarily mean you are home free. You still have hard work ahead of you. You constantly need new pictures, you always have to get to your appointments on time, keep your weight in check, make sure you have enough composites with you at all times for your castings, drag around a portfolio to all of your castings, still go on your appointments even after being sick, or spending all night at a club, or getting lost in another country, or getting stuck in traffic. You *still* have to look refreshed, have a smile on your face, as well as be in a good mood when you meet the client or arrive at a job first thing in the morning.

After you arrive at your job or test shoot you may have to stand for several hours in one place under hot lights with people pulling at your clothes and telling you how to stand. The hair and makeup crew could arrange your hair in a scalp-tightening "'do" that takes you an hour to take down after you get home, and put a ton of makeup on your face over and over again as the day wears on and your sweat starts to mix in with your foundation, which eventually gives you acne . . . and this may all have to be done in shoes that are two sizes too small for your feet. A model from Ford just recently showed up at a fashion show that I was casting for New York Fashion Show Week, and her feet were ripped up and bleeding from wearing brand-new stilettos for so many days in a row to castings without stockings. The designer asked her to walk across the room in high-heeled shoes that he gave her so he could envision her in his show, and after patching up her feet with Band-Aids, she bravely took a few steps, even though she was in intense pain. Looking professional is not enough—you also have to act professional, which can take a great deal of patience at times.

In the end, having a successful modeling career is highly rewarding. And if you start working regularly, the benefits can be amazing, such as the money, travel, and meeting people from all corners of the world. But I just want you to be aware of what lies ahead for you when you become a model. Most of the cushy jobs won't start coming your way until you have established yourself in the industry, which takes time. And even then, there will be some clients who treat you like a product and not a human being. If you brace yourself for hard work and realize that a modeling career doesn't start overnight, then you are ready to begin selling yourself as a professional model. One of the biggest mistakes that models make once they have an agency is thinking they are home free, but that is really only the beginning of where an exciting career can take you—if you stick with it through all of the many ups and downs it may bring you.

SCAMS AND SCHOOLS

At first I was only going to include a few pages on scams and schools, but when I started researching what you need to know about scams, and combined it with what I already know and have experienced, I couldn't resist letting you in on the sordid details of the scams that take place constantly in the world of modeling. I felt that you deserved an entire chapter on this subject, as much as you may not want to think you will be a target for a scam. My whole rationale in writing this book was to show people like you how to break in to the modeling industry for *limited or no money*, and modeling scams are the biggest way people lose their money.

Scams

I have mentioned to you before (and probably will again before the end of this book) that when you pay money up front to someone who claims they will market you in this business, or to a photographer who is not affiliated with the industry, it is *completely* unnecessary. Let's get this straight: paying an amateur photographer money for taking pictures is not a scam, but it *is* a scam if a photographer tells you that his or her pictures are necessary for finding representation, or he or she leads you to believe that their pictures will help you better find an agency. A scam isn't someone scouting you to be a model, but it *is* when he or she charges you money up front and makes you think they are part of a legitimate modeling agency. A scam isn't a modeling competition, but it *is* when you pay upward of $1,000 to be in a modeling competition when there was never any chance of you winning, or the judges who attended the contest were bogus.

PHOTOGRAPHY SCAMS

There are several different ways to be taken advantage of in regards to photography. These include purchasing "photo packages" from photographers when you do not need them (or when the photographer is not at least affiliated with a modeling agency), as well as how a model is treated on an actual photo shoot. Though photography scams are very common they are a topic that is rarely addressed when a new model enters the modeling industry.

Before we go on, I feel that it is crucial to mention that most photographers are not scam artists. But there are enough of them out there that I feel I have to warn you. Photographers become the "directors" of a photo shoot, and when you feel that you need pictures—or you are made to feel that way through high-pressure sales tactics—it's easy to be sucked into purchasing useless pictures or doing something on set that you will regret in the long run.

Paying for photo packages or pictures for a portfolio is the most common mistake that people make who are not yet represented by an agency. I have been saying throughout this book that professional pictures are completely unnecessary to have when searching for an agency. And modeling agencies actually *prefer* nonprofessional pictures when a person is trying to gain representation from an agency. People spend hundreds, often *thousands* of dollars unnecessarily for professional pictures before they join an agency. When I was a modeling agent, a mother came in with her daughter carrying a portfolio, and she told me she spent over $10,000 on the pictures. I didn't have the heart to tell her that she didn't need to do that, and that her daughter was never going to be a high-fashion model. They could have saved the plane ticket and hotel in New York, plus the $10,000, and sent digital pictures by e-mail to me, and I would have told them the same thing. Or the mother and daughter could have just flown to New York and gone on open calls (without *any* professional pictures of her), and they would have gotten the same response for a lot less money.

In addition to selling useless pictures, nonreputable *and reputable* photographers sometimes take sexual advantage of a model posing for a photo shoot. I have experienced as well as heard stories about photographers trying to get models to do things they don't want to do, like take off their tops, undress fully in front of the camera, or pose in ways that make them uncomfortable. There is a fine line between clothed photo shoots and other types of modeling, and the way to judge if you are in an unsavory situation is to figure out if you are comfortable with what is going on, or not.

America and other countries' views toward nudity can be very different, so you may feel that you are being taken advantage of even when you really aren't. For example, sunbathing topless in a public place is a common occurrence in Europe, though it is considered to be indecent exposure over here in the United States. Also, the difference is quite apparent in magazines and advertising in America as opposed to Europe and other countries. Nudity is taken much more casually in other countries than in the States. What does this have to do with you going on a photo shoot? Well, I feel that I need to point out that foreign models and photographers sometimes have a more casual way of looking at nudity than Americans do. A foreign model may not find it a big deal at all to take off her top in front of the camera, whereas an American model may be uncomfortable if asked to do this. And it's not just the females who are preyed upon; male models are targets as well. Nude modeling is a common occurrence in the industry, and perhaps— when you're ready—you'll be prepared to make a choice that you'll feel comfortable with in the long run. Just because the girl or guy next to you is ready to disrobe at a moment's notice does not mean you have to, *ever,* if you are not completely at ease in doing so. Plus, if you participate in something you do not want to do in front of the camera, it will show all over your face in the pictures. Know the saying, "a picture is worth a thousand words"? Well, if you are feeling insecure about something, a picture can be worth more than a thousand words, *and* be released on the Internet someday. To sum it all up, you could get caught in a situation that isn't considered to be a big deal to someone, but it is to *you,* and you should always stand your ground and be comfortable with everything that you do on a photo shoot, no matter what the situation, or who is shooting the pictures.

You may also feel that you are *not* being taken advantage of when you really are. Some situations that come up may have been staged on purpose, and you should be prepared for those as well. Stories of corrupt photographers keep finding their way back to me over and over again, through channels that I would never imagine. I was getting my hair done by Andrew John, a former celebrity hairstylist in the fashion and television industry. He said that he was approached by a photographer, who was referred by a friend, who wanted Andrew to solicit some of the high-fashion models whose hair he styled to see if they would come to his studio for a photo shoot. "Why would I do this?" Andrew said to me. "I told him to go through the proper channels by approaching a modeling agency, showing them his book, and having the agency decide if they would give him models or not, and after that I never heard from him again." So no matter who is approaching you for a photo shoot, whether it is someone in the fashion industry, your hairstylist, or a well-meaning friend, be careful to have the photographer checked out thoroughly, or at least get a reference from someone, such as a model he or she has worked with in the past. This is *especially* important in the case of amateur photographers, whether a modeling agency works with him or her or not. If a photographer chooses not to go through an agency to find models for testing then either they have been rejected by all the agencies because their work is not good enough for a model portfolio, or they are scam artists. The photographer doesn't necessarily have to be asking for money either. When photographers solicit unrepresented models, some of them just like having beautiful girls or handsome guys in their studio so they can prey on them sexually. As I said before, there are a lot of reputable photographers out there, but there are also a few who you need to watch out for.

How can you be sure about whether a test photographer is going to treat you right? Unfortunately it is difficult, but you can start by checking their references from modeling agencies and other models who have worked with him or her. When I was a model, photographers made sexual advances toward me on *legitimate photo shoots for reputable clients*! Hopefully, since you are warned about this ahead of time, you will be more prepared to deal with the situation if it happens. That is a great reason not to procure work without an agency—you will have no one to call and help you deal with an unsavory situation such as sexual harassment. Modeling agencies try to protect their models as best they can, legally, financially, and emotionally, and it is in your best interest to get work *and* professional pictures through a legitimate modeling agency.

WEB SITE SCAMS

Web site scams are based on the same fact that I have been repeating throughout this entire book: *if you are paying money up front to try and break into the modeling industry, it is not a legitimate way to get into the business*. There is no other way around it! Any reputable modeling agency that is involved in the industry will support this statement—there are no shortcuts to becoming a model that you have to pay for. If someone charges you to be on their Web site, and it is not the Web site of a legitimate, or backed by a legitimate, modeling agency, then it is more than likely a scam. And be careful—some Web sites put the logos of well-known modeling agencies on their site to trick you, and the real agencies are not even aware that the site exists.

Most modeling agencies have Web sites of their models, and they have to charge monthly fees and upkeep, but first of all, they will not charge a fee up front for this service before you are with the agency, and second of all, that is one of the most popular ways to market an agency these days. When someone is trying to convince you to pay them to put you on their Web site and they are not an agency, it is not the proper way to do business. People will tell you that clients are doing searches on the Web site for models, and agencies are always looking for potential models on those sites, and most of that just isn't true. There are too many specialized managers, scouts, and agencies to give these clients what they need without them having to go look for it themselves. If a Web site *does* have clients searching for new faces, most likely they will be agencies you have never heard of or offer jobs that will not pay nearly as much as if you got them through an established agency. You will fare much better as a model by sending the pictures that I taught you to take in to modeling agencies, because that way you will be most protected by going through a legitimate agency. Web sites that a manager sets up are different—they will have a Web site, even though they are not an agency and don't have specific jobs for you, because they are trying to market you to agencies around the world. But again, they will not charge you *ahead* of time to be on their site, and monthly maintenance fees should be minimal, around twenty dollars a month.

A friend of mine signed up on one of the Internet-based companies that claimed they could "start your career" as a model, and they asked that a bunch of personal information, along with her pictures, be submitted into their registry. My friend purposely did not attach her pictures, just to see what the company would do, and they called her every other day wanting her to come in for an "interview" until she told them it was the wrong number. They said it didn't matter what she looked like, she had the measurements of a high-fashion model, and they could get her started with just a one-time fee. *It doesn't matter what someone "looks like"?* I thought that the modeling industry was *based* on looks! It is true that commercial print and acting work are much more open to a broader range of types than high-fashion modeling, but it certainly takes more than just posting your pictures on an Internet site to break into this business. One of the Web sites that I found in my research even claimed that if you "click here" you would become a model! Not unless a genie bottle flew out of the computer, that's for sure.

I am giving you so many details about all of these kinds of scams because I really want you to both know what to look for when you're trying to break into this business, and protect yourself against scam artists when it involves chasing your dream. Even if you do not become the success you thought you would be in the modeling business, at least you will not have wasted your money. If you have already been caught in something similar to what I described, just cancel your subscription or don't pay any more money to anyone from here on out. If you feel you have been wronged, contact the Better Business Bureau in your area and report them. It is *so* easy to be sucked into a high-pressure sales pitch that zeroes in on your dream. There are people out there who prey on parents of children wanting to be models, as well as people who would like to be models themselves. This is why I am so happy that you are taking the time to read this book!

MODEL CONVENTIONS AND COMPETITIONS

The marketing strategy in this book reaches out to a much wider audience than any convention company can within a short weekend, with thousands of models attending and limited clients on their roster. You should know that modeling conventions usually have three thousand to five thousand people attending, with only twenty to thirty modeling agents from around the world scouting. The possibility of you getting "discovered" at these events is very small. Even if there are a *hundred* modeling agents and scouts there (and that's a lot), the chance of every one of those agents seeing every face of the thousands of wannabe models in one weekend is slim. Do you really think that is how you can get discovered? From my experience as a judge at these events, after seeing fifty or so people everyone starts to look the same, especially if there are *thousands* of contestants, which there usually are.

The only thing you are missing that this book can't give you is walking a live runway in front of some bored agents and clients—clients who may not even be associated with the fashion industry! *Many times convention companies claim that a judge is from a big-name company in the fashion or entertainment industry, while in reality he or she is only a receptionist or an office assistant for that company.* These people have *no say* in the final choices for talent or model representation within their company but go for the free trips and per diems that are offered to them. That is the way modeling conventions or competitions get clients to judge or scout models; they offer clients free airfare, hotel, and spending money to warm-weather destinations. Don't get caught up in this scene by high-pressure sales, *especially* if you can't afford it. I *promise* you, paying out money to someone to get your start in the modeling business is absolutely unnecessary.

Plenty of modeling agencies host *legitimate* contests you can enter for free; but don't expect to get accepted so easily because they are not charging you anything. Think about it—the conventions that take money from you are going to take money from *anyone . . . you are basically paying them to sign you up no matter how small or nonexistent your chances are.* There may be an "interview" or a request to see your pictures, but state laws that governed a convention company I personally worked for proclaimed that the company was not a "modeling agency" and therefore could not be discriminatory against anyone. This means they will take your money even if they know you have *no chance at all.* It's a loophole that makes scamming you out of your money legal!

The agencies in the past that have presented *legitimate* types of contests are:

Ford Models: "Ford Supermodel of the World"
Elite Models: "Elite Model Look"
New York Model Management: *Make Me a Supermodel* show
Next Model Management
Wilhelmina Models: many contests, each run in tandem with a
    magazine or sponsor of some sort

These agencies—and there are many more, including modeling agencies abroad—pay for all or most expenses for the finalist models competing in their contests, and some of these events have taken place in such countries as Ecuador, China, India, United States, Dominican Republic, and all over the world.

Several national magazines have also done model searches in the past, such as *Sports Illustrated* for their swimsuit edition, *Cosmo Girl*, *Cosmopolitan, Men's Health* magazine for the cover, *Glamour, Seventeen, Prom, More* for their over-forty female model search, and I'm sure many others hold model searches on a consistent basis, and will probably do so again. Some of the model competitions charge a nominal fee to process the paperwork, but it's worth it, especially because more and more magazines are using "real" people for their photo shoots and will access their applicants from a database to call in for possible shoots. But do not pay any more than around twenty-five dollars or so, and then only if the company is legitimate, such as when New York Models sponsors a competition with a magazine, or a magazine like *More* sponsors a competition with a modeling agency. Just constantly utilize the search engines on the Internet and you will find new ones popping up all the time. But once again, be careful about whom you submit any personal information to, even your e-mail address.

IF YOU ARE APPROACHED BY SOMEONE WHO SAYS YOU SHOULD BE A MODEL

My teenage readers, picture this: you're at the shopping mall, an amusement park, or a rock concert, and someone comes up to you and says, "Excuse me, are you a model?" How flattering! And if you're older than a teenager, you will get a similar spiel in a different setting: you may be attending college, walking down the street in a larger city, or in a mall shopping as well—malls are very popular for scam artists. They are not stupid—you come to the mall to spend money, right? And there are hordes of people caught off guard to choose from at a shopping mall. Someone approaches you and says, "Have you ever thought about modeling?" If anyone comes up to you in a public place and says you should be a model, there are specific questions you must ask them, and make sure you get the answers. The following questions are what you need to ask, how the person should answer, and why you need to know these things.

1. **ARE YOU A SCOUT?** The answer to this question should be a simple yes. If the person that approached you is not a scout, then the answer of "agent" or "manager" is acceptable. If anyone gives you an answer that is different from one of those three, politely excuse yourself and leave. Then go buy something nice for yourself with all of the money you saved by not spending it on a scam! But do be careful, because there were scam artists at one point who used the term "scout" when

approaching people on the street, but later had to tell their employees to stop using that term because it created trouble for potential customers checking up on them. People would call agencies to ask if someone was "scouting" for them on the street and charging such-and-such price, and all of the agencies had the same answer—NO. If anyone is trying to charge you something, or get you into their offices for an "interview," don't bother. If someone is a true "scout" then they will also have satisfactory answers to the next questions I give you.

2. **WHAT AGENCY OR AGENCIES ARE YOU AFFILIATED WITH?** A lot of scouts or managers work with several different agencies all over the world. They should be able to give you references from agencies to verify their credibility. A scout who works for one particular agency full time should be able to produce a business card with their agency's logo on it, and the company's full name and phone number. *Check these people out thoroughly!* Call all the references they give you, ask about their reputation, and go online and check the agencies' Web sites that the scout or manager mentioned to you. Also search their name and/or their company's name in Google or Yahoo!, as scams tend to get put online pretty quickly as warnings, and you may be able to find out something about the person if he or she is not reputable. Another good way to check out someone is to get a phone number of a model who has already been working with him or her—it is all in the name of good business tactics as well as safety. Get all this information and check on every one of their references *before* giving away any personal information, *even your first name!*

3. **IS THERE ANY FEE INVOLVED?** If there is *any* charge to you, that person is not legitimate. I'm sorry to keep repeating this, but it really is the whole premise of the most popular scam for breaking into modeling. If you get one thing out of this book, I hope it is the fact that you do not have to pay anyone money to enter into the modeling business. If they have the right

contacts for you to get an agency or manager, they will work it out with whoever signs you on by taking a percentage *from the agency* of what you make, or charging a one-time finder's fee *to the agency*. **Do not let this question go unanswered!!** Many times scam artists will try to dodge this particular question just to get you into their offices. Then they set up their office space to give the illusion they are an affluent modeling agency or something that is at least legitimate and successful. I have been to the most luxurious offices, including the penthouse office of a billionaire executive, that were full of professional scam artists—who were actually ex-cons—working behind the scenes. Of course, I didn't realize it at the time—they put on a good show! But that's just what it was—a show that sucked people in to spend all their money on nothing.

DO YOUR RESEARCH AND GET REFERRALS

You can easily research a company's name by using the Google search engine, at www.google.com, or going to the Better Business Bureau's site, at www.bbb.org, and looking for complaints against the company, or by calling the BBB to see if they have complaints against them, or simply by asking for referrals from other agencies in a different market. Modeling agencies are always communicating with one another around the world, and agencies are constantly proposing models to other agencies—especially if they are the model's manager or mother agent—to get them placed with agencies in other markets. Also, when a model leaves a market, an agency is still proposing him or her for certain jobs, so the model's current agency needs to tell the agency in the market they are going to next what potential work the model may have, so there are no double bookings, which means having jobs scheduled in two different places at the same time. Agencies *are required* to work with other agencies; there is no choice. So referrals from other legitimate modeling agencies are a good way to do your research on the reputation of an agency. An example of what I am talking about is when a model from New York goes to Paris temporarily to try and work during their fashion show season, then comes back to New York because it is his or her home base. The agencies in New York and Paris need to communicate frequently on what the model is doing, because jobs from New York may overlap during the time the model should be in Paris, or he/she may receive more work offers extending until way after the shows in Paris are over, in which case the French agency would have to call New York and consult about the possibility of the model staying longer. My point is that agencies know other agencies quite well, and it's a good way to research the legitimacy of some of them. Smaller agencies in tiny markets may be harder to find out about, but your key hint is that there will be no money charged to you up front for *anything*!

TAKE ACTION

If you feel that you have been approached with a scam, please contact your state's attorney general's office, or the local Consumer Protection Agency, or the Better Business Bureau. The only way that these con artists will learn their lesson not to prey on people's dreams will be if the public stands up to them and reports what they are doing. Too many scam artists fly under the radar simply because there are no clear-cut definitions on how people should enter into the modeling industry, or what kind of things the public should look out for when approached by someone who says they are in the modeling industry. Perhaps if enough people publicly voice their outrage about being taken advantage of, then lawmakers will sit up and take notice. Don't wait until these companies make more and more money off of innocent victims. Report unsavory situations as soon as you feel that someone is trying to take advantage of you. No one should have to succumb to high-pressure sales when it comes to pursuing their dream. You need to take classes and invest money to break into areas of the entertainment industry such as music, dancing, singing, or acting—with the exception of commercials where you don't have to speak. But you do *not* need to spend money to break into the modeling industry *before* you get representation. So don't fall into any of those traps, and spread the word to your friends on the way it really is.

IT'S YOUR CHOICE

After all is said and done, if you have extra money lying around and *still* want to be in a staged modeling competition, go for a company that at least has a reputable name in the fashion industry and brings in legit clients, managers, and agents to be judges for the competition, such as a company like Pro Scout. But go into it with no preconceptions, and have fun. Most likely that's all you will get out of it, especially if you are reading this book before you go, because I tell you everything they will, and a whole lot more. I even hosted workshops at these events, giving people tips on the "how to's" of modeling, so I know everything that the convention companies would teach you.

Modeling Schools

Modeling schools are not considered to be scams because they provide you with classes and workshops that you pay for, as you would for any specialized school, but once again, these classes will not tell you anything more than what is contained in this book. A modeling school does not select you—*you select them*. They will let *anyone* pay them (much like a convention company) to "teach" someone how to be a "model." Save your money, unless it is something you can afford and are not expecting anything more out of it than good posture tips and makeup lessons. Yes, there are a few people that have gotten "discovered" out of modeling schools, but not many. And those models who went on to have successful careers could have started modeling for free, because a modeling school does just what I am teaching you to do, but you will learn even more in the process. When you tell a modeling agent that you have been to a modeling school, it does not at all change your chances of being taken on by the agency. Modeling schools are considered to be a waste of money by most agencies, except for the ones that are associated with them, of course, because they get a percentage of the profits.

Modeling schools are sometimes associated with a legitimate modeling *agency* . . . so you can be with that agency if you sign up for the school. But the catch is that you can still present your pictures to that agency anyway, even if you are not signed up with the school! Don't let the way things are presented to you make up your mind to spend money in this business. If something seems too good to be true, then it probably is. The only exception to that is if an agency advances you money for expenses such as a plane ticket or hotel fee. That may seem like a dream come true, but remember that it is an *advance*, which means you still have to pay that money back eventually. And it's only an amazing offer if the agency is *reputable*.

Remember, I am trying to get you involved in the modeling business the *best* and most economical way. If you *want* to spend all your money it's up to you. But I promise you, if you exhaust all the opportunities this book presents to you, then *you are* giving it your all. Doling out money to people who cannot help you nearly as much as I can, or to people who have no intention of helping you after taking your money, is completely unnecessary.

The Universal Rule

I sat down with Capucine Catsets, former head scout of Elite Models in Los Angeles and Miami for twenty-one years, and she agreed with me that the number of scams out there and the amount of dollars wasted on those scams is horrifying. It's not a question of how much *money* you have; it's a question of how much *potential* you have. She expressed to me that it's so difficult to scout these days, with the abundance of scammers who charge people incredible amounts of money for no reason. All of the scouts and agents I spoke to when I was writing this book wish there could be some sort of understanding, once and for all, about the proper way to enter into the modeling industry. For all agencies that are legitimate, the number one rule in the modeling business is: You do not need to pay money to break into the modeling industry. But it's the one rule that people just do not understand or follow.

Various modeling agents around the world whom I have told about this book made me promise to warn you about giving too much personal information to someone who approaches you in public. Anyone can print up a business card with A, B, or C Management on it and give it to you to look official, as well as buy a domain name for fifteen dollars and put up a Web site to appear legitimate, along with an e-mail address for the site. It is *your* responsibility to check out that person thoroughly before you begin a relationship with them, and not get fooled by any outward appearances that *seem* legitimate.

Unfortunately, there are always going to be different kinds of scams in the modeling industry that people create to trick unknowing consumers, as is the case in every industry. The advantage that you have now is you know how to avoid these people, check references, and not fall for high-pressure sales tactics, especially when it involves money. In addition, you should try not to put yourself in situations where you feel the least bit uncomfortable, whether it be at a photo shoot or if you are being charged for something up front without the involvement of a legitimate agency. If that happens, just remove yourself from the situation physically, and move on from there. Just walk away! You have the right to take your time with anything, particularly when paying someone money.

When people have big dreams it is easy to believe someone is going to help you, especially if they are presenting a quick and easy route to your goal. Just remember, there is no quick and easy in this business, it takes hard work and patience for long-term success. Don't listen to anyone who tries to sell you stardom for a price; if someone can make you a "star" then they will be able to do it *the right way, without charging you before you get with an agency*! If you could buy stardom, then there would be a lot more people doing it. Concentrate on getting the proper representation, and let the modeling agencies do the work of making you a "star."

BUSINESS TIPS,
TERMS TO KNOW, AND
A WORD TO PARENTS

One of the most important things I hope you have learned so far from reading this book is that modeling is a business, albeit a more glamorous business than others, but still a business. You have to pay your taxes and perhaps take deductions, sign legal contracts, and manage yourself accordingly. This chapter will clue you in on some of the administrative details that you will need to know about the modeling industry. From your income taxes to signing contracts, I will provide you some business tips that I have learned along the way, as well as give you additional advice to help get you started once you find representation. I have also included a few terms you should know to help better protect yourself when finding your way around the modeling industry. And this chapter also contains some advice for parents that I, as a parent myself, feel you should be made aware of. I wish someone had told me these things when I first started modeling! I will also show you a few things about how to manage your child's career more responsibly, now and in the long run.

Modeling Is a Business

I was very impressed with seventeen-year-old Elma, a high-fashion model in New York City, who stated that "modeling is a business, just like all of the other arts. The trick is to combine the creative side with the sales, similar to how painters or musicians do. You should open yourself up to all the creativity that modeling has to offer, while still keeping an organized, efficiently run business for yourself. If artists only painted or sang and did not treat their craft as a serious business, then no one would know they exist, and it is the same for working as a model." Elma had just begun her modeling career when she said this to me, but had already grasped the concept of managing herself as a business entity.

KEEP THOSE RECEIPTS

The one thing that I wish I had known from the very start of my modeling career—even before I had representation at an agency—was that I should keep *all* my receipts. Keep receipts for everything that you do. You would be surprised at the number of tax write-offs you are legally allowed to have in the fashion industry. Any accountant who has experience doing models' taxes can give you a checklist of categories that you can claim as write-offs on your taxes. Just put the receipts in a large envelope or folder, and then sort them out at the end of the year according to the checklist that you obtained. Even if you do not make any money the first year you are modeling or trying to break in, you can still claim certain expenses on your taxes, depending, of course, on what other work you procured. You should research this with an accountant who knows the law. But though I am not an accountant, I can give you some examples of potential write-offs: the gas you used to drive to an open call, stamps you put on your mailings, clothing, makeup, film for your camera, apartment rent if you temporarily moved somewhere to start or continue your career, computer expenses, and so much more can all be tax deductions. Again, contact an accountant for a complete list because the deductions add up quickly!

TAXES, WORKING ABROAD,
AND FOREIGN MODELS

Taxes, taxes, taxes . . . unfortunately, taxes are *not* taken out of your paycheck as a model, unless the client happens to be paying through a payroll company, which is very rare in this business. I say "unfortunately" because so many models get stuck with a huge tax bill in April without any warning and have put no money aside for it. You need to set up with the Internal Revenue Service a quarterly payment plan for estimated taxes so you do not get blindsided at tax time. This is actually a requirement for people who are self-employed, such as models, and who expect to pay more than $1,000 a year in taxes. The payment plan is also a great way to put away your money for that lump sum in April. *Foreign models* will have taxes taken out of their model bookings, but Americans do not.

If you are an American citizen and you work overseas, you will have taxes taken out from your pay, just as the foreigners do here, and depending on how long you are out of the country, you may only have to pay taxes abroad. But if you are not out of the country for long enough, you still have to file all of your income (domestic and foreign) over here in the States.

Keep detailed accounts of any money made overseas. You may be able to also use receipts for write-offs from over there. Again, see an accountant to figure out your financial status! I know quite a bit about the modeling industry but do not claim to be an expert regarding the government's regulations. I am just trying to give you a heads-up so you can follow through with what is expected of you.

While we are on the subject of overseas work, foreign models need visas to work in the States. If you are a foreign model then you need an agency to sponsor you. That agency can then submit the paperwork for you. From my experience of working with foreign models in the United States, there is a temporary (three months) visa an agency can get to have a model come to the States. It is called the B1 visa. Here is how it works: a modeling agency (from the United States) that represents a model overseas who wants to come and check out a particular market, needs to send the model a "letter of invitation" stating that they are inviting him or her over to the United States to see clients *only*. This temporary visa does *not* allow the model to work whatsoever. The agency that invites a particular model here to the States will have to promise to pay for the model's airfare and accommodations, and will ensure that the model returns to his or her home country within the three-month time period. This is expressly for having a model meet clients to see how professionals in the modeling industry respond to him or her to decide if it is worth it for the model to pursue a career in the United States. The model is not allowed to work with this particular visa, but if he or she gets a positive reaction from the agency's clients, then the agency may want to look into a more permanent visa (meaning three years in length) to sponsor the model and help him or her reside in this country.

A common visa for work that models try to obtain is an H-1B visa. An H-1B is a standard visa that most models use to apply for work in the States. There is also the O1 visa, which is a highly specialized visa that more accomplished models or entertainers in their field can submit an application for, but you need to have representation first. An O1 visa requires a minimum of fifty tear sheets for a model, and if he or she has originals of press coverage or tear sheets from magazines to go with that. Reference letters from established companies are also required from the model's home country for both kinds of visas. It is a lot of work getting together all that paperwork, and costly as well. Visas can cost upward of $2,000, including lawyer's expenses and government fees. And the application process can take up to six months after you submit your claim, even if you can get your application in through the correct channels; and even with all that, there is still a small chance of denial.

CONTRACTS

When you are offered a contractual agreement, please read everything that an agency wants you to sign, and preferably get a lawyer to look it over if you can. Tell the agency you would like to bring it home and read it—this is perfectly acceptable. You have to legally be eighteen years old for a contract to be valid, so if you are younger, your parents or legal guardian will have to sign it for you. Take your time reading these documents, because some of them will tie you up for years at a time, with exclusive rights possibly going to that particular agency *worldwide* involving your future work.

Most of the modeling agencies have standard contracts, but you should fully understand what you are signing anyway, especially because there are a few agencies out there that will try to be deceitful. You should also completely grasp the concept of the difference between "agency" and "manager," and the definition of "mother agent" before you sign an agreement with anyone that states that term in what you are signing. I go into this in more detail under "Terms You Should Know" in this chapter. Some of the agencies won't mention that being your "mother agent" is in their contract, so do go over the whole agreement meticulously *before* you sign.

A modeling agency will also ask for a "power of attorney" from you in a contract. There is no need to ask for this if they are not an accredited agency, because only an agency has the legal right to book work for you, as opposed to a manager. "Power of attorney" means that you are giving them permission to sign your signature on your behalf. Sound scary? This is necessary because companies will most often pay the agency in your name, and the agency needs to cash the check, take their percentage out, and then give you your money. This is a common procedure. To protect yourself, just make sure the power of attorney is limited to modeling work, or anything having to do with your modeling career.

The time limit of a contract is negotiable. Most of the contracts state three years as the contract's life span, and then every year after that it is automatically renewed unless one of the parties terminates the agreement in writing. You can knock that number down to one or two years, but it's up to you. I wouldn't worry about "term" lengths though unless you are in high fashion, because a model's career in high fashion should be handled very carefully, and if an agency you are with is not being strategic with your career, you may want to change agencies after a while. Plus, a high-fashion model has a chance at possibly becoming a supermodel, and the less tied down you are, the better, because you will have more negotiating power in the long run.

Do not let an agency intimidate you into signing a contract before you have read it, or before you have entirely researched the company. Stand your ground, take it home, think about it, and make sure you are comfortable committing to both the agency and the contract. If the agency is legitimate, they will give you as much time as you need, *but* don't expect to get advances for anything or go on appointments for work if you do not have that contract signed and given back to them.

Contracts vary from agency to agency, but I've condensed a standard agency contract in order for you to get an idea of what one looks like. You will be asked to sign something like this if an agency wants to represent you exclusively.

ABC MODEL AGENCY

This letter shall constitute an agreement between (*agency name*) hereinafter referred to as "Manager," and (*model's name*), hereinafter referred to as "Talent," as follows:

1. Talent hereby engages Manager's services and Manager accepts such engagement as Talent's sole and exclusive (*area or city*) manager for the term of this Agreement in the field of modeling, entertainment, and runway. As such, Manager shall: advise and counsel Talent in any and all matters regarding publicity and public relations and the general practices of the modeling, entertainment, and advertising industries; advise and counsel Talent regarding the proper formats for presenting Talent to third parties, including but not limited to aspects of makeup, hair, photo composites and formation of portfolio.

2. Talent hereby appoints Manager as lawful Attorney-in-Fact and grants Manager power of attorney to collect and receive monies on Talent's behalf, to endorse Talent's name upon and deposit same in Manager's account with any bank, and to retain there from all sums due Manager at any time. Talent also authorizes Manager to approve and permit the use of Talent's name, photograph, likeness and voice and sign releases on Talent's behalf.

3. Talent agrees to seek Manager's counsel in regard to all matters concerning Talent's endeavors in the field of modeling and entertainment. Talent shall advise Manager of all offers of assignments submitted to Talent with respect to modeling and will refer any inquiries concerning Talent's services to Manager.

4. In consideration of entering into this agreement and as compensation for the services to be rendered by Manager hereunder, Talent agrees to pay Manager an amount equal to twenty percent (20%) of any and all gross monies or other consideration which Talent receives as a result of agreements (and any renewals or renegotiations thereof) relating to Talent's modeling throughout the world as procured by Manager, which agreements are entered into during the term hereof. In addition, Talent agrees to pay Manager an amount equal to ten percent (10%) of any and all gross monies derived from any (SAG or AFTRA) union-regulated television commercials, industrials, uses and/or renewal fees as applicable. Talent agrees to pay or reimburse Manager for all out-of-pocket expenses which Manager incurs from time to time on behalf of Talent.

5. Talent is aware and agrees that Manager is entitled to receive a service charge from any and all of the clients who utilize Talent's services.

6. The Talent represents and warrants that the Talent is under no disability, restriction or prohibition with respect to the Talent's right to execute this Agreement and perform its terms and conditions.

7. The term of this agreement shall be a period of three (3) years commencing as of the date below, and it will be automatically renewed for three (3) years at a time unless Manager or Talent gives written notice to the other of the intention to terminate by registered mail at least ninety (90) days prior to the end of the then current term.

Agreed and accepted:
(Agency name)
(Agency officer's signature)
(Model's name, address, etc.)
(Model's signature, if eighteen years or older)

UNFORESEEN EXPENSES

There are plenty of expenses that a modeling agency will charge without your prior approval. This is standard practice in the industry, but it is a big reason why you should keep track of your expenses very carefully. You should request monthly statements because there are sometimes mistakes made in accounting. Don't be afraid or embarrassed to ask for an explanation of your statements or charges either—the people working there are only human, and it is a good idea to double-check their figures constantly. Some modeling agencies let you do more on your own, as far as printing composites and such, but other agencies want to keep a more uniform image, so they have in-house printing and an art department to do that for you, and it's all added to your "account" (the money that you owe them) and charged against your future earnings without your prior approval.

What are some of these "expenses" I keep talking about? Well, I have mentioned a few along the way, but the more common ones that you will regularly be charged for are: composite cards, agency portfolio, monthly Web site maintenance fees, retouching on pictures from photo shoots, laser copies of pictures, messenger fees, postage, Polaroid pictures taken of you in the agency, overnight mailings, and agency advertising (like an agency poster or book). Models may make a great amount of money per day, but there are a *ton* of marketing costs *after* your commission and taxes are taken out of your check!

When you first join an agency, they will probably take Polaroid or digital pictures of you to make a "Polaroid sheet." This sheet will consist of a head shot, a three-quarter shot, profile, and/or a full-length body shot, all done with a Polaroid or digital camera. Sometimes an agency will have the body shots on a separate sheet, with you in a bathing suit. Does this sound familiar? (If not, read chapter 2 again at a slower pace and note the similarities between these photos and the ones I taught you to take.) The Polaroid sheet is for the clients who request your nonprofessional pictures. Some clients *prefer* Polaroids or digital pictures to portfolios, but most ask for them in addition to your portfolio. Also, clients who book work without seeing you first (called direct bookings) want to see Polaroid or digital images of you so they can see how you look outside your portfolio pictures in a more natural setting, without makeup and overstyled hair, much as you would appear to them in person on a casting call or go-see. Also, when you cut or dye your hair, or lose weight, the agency has to take new pictures of you for marketing purposes, because suddenly you no longer look like the pictures in your portfolio, and Polaroids or digitals give the clients an idea of how you have changed until you can get new test pictures in your book. Some agencies will charge you up to $1.50 a picture for Polaroid pictures, and *will not ask for your prior approval.*

Your agency will also make several color laser copies of your portfolio to have in the agency so when a client requests a hard copy of your book, the agency can messenger or overnight express it right away, and the charges for that are the laser copies that they need to make on your behalf, as well as the costs to get it to the client. Some of the larger agencies do their marketing primarily digitally, but I know in New York City the clients quite frequently still want to see hard copies of models' portfolios.

The other hidden charges I listed are mostly marketing materials the agency incurs on your behalf, except for the retouching fees that are charged for the pictures in your portfolio. These fees depend on how much time the person retouching your face or body has to spend in doing this. Retouched pictures can range from taking a pimple off of your face to filling in bathing suit strap marks to changing the shape of your nose—it's amazing what they can do! My point, though, is that agencies can find a lot to charge you with in this area and will do so without your input unless you let them know that you want to be involved. You can get estimates about the costs of this kind of work before it's done though, as opposed to something like a messenger fee, where you have to trust the agency a little more in their estimate of how much to charge you. (Sometimes portfolios go out in a group and the fee is split different ways, and other times you have to pay for only *your* portfolio to go to a client, which is more expensive.)

Finally, *always* keep in touch with an agency's accounting department! It is *your* money, and they should be happy to answer any and all of your questions at any time—including how they charge messenger and postal fees. Usually there is a log of detailed expenses that are charged to a model's account, and you can see exactly what was charged to you, and when it was charged. After you get representation, the marketing for modeling work can be expensive, depending on what market you are in and the type of model that you are, and should be monitored carefully.

Know Your Terminology

Getting an agency to represent you is not the only thing you need to know how to do. You also need to protect yourself from people who try to take advantage of you *after* you enter the industry, and knowing the terms or lingo of the business will help you with that. If you get representation, that's amazing! But you should not let down your guard when you actually enter the industry as a new model. Keep your eyes and ears wide open, because there are agencies that will try and take advantage of you—especially when it comes to money. By the time you are asked to sign a contract with an agency, you should know these terms and you will more or less have the background you need to begin your career.

The following list of terms should be read over carefully to further guard yourself by knowing the business inside and out. Refer back to this list when people start using this terminology with you in the business, or when they ask you to sign something with these words or phrases in it. I didn't make a glossary of terms, because I felt like the lingo that you should know requires not only a definition but an explanation as well. You will especially want to know this valuable information before you sign *any* kind of agreement or contract. Knowing these terms will help you bridge the gap between breaking into the modeling industry and actually signing a contract with an agency. Remember, it's a business, and you need to arm yourself with the knowledge of how everything works on the business end of the modeling industry.

TERMS YOU SHOULD KNOW

MOTHER AGENCY

This is the agency or manager who discovered you; he or she gets to make the final decisions in your career over all other agencies and will help you progress in your career for as long as your agreement lasts. Every other agency will have to get permission from the mother agency first to book you. For example, if you are discovered in Europe, and you move to New York, your European mother agency will oversee your career in New York, if they are an active mother agent. If your agency in New York has a huge campaign for you, and your mother agency in Europe does not think you should do it because it is not the right type of exposure for you, then the agency in New York has to respect their decision. And it could go the other way as well—if a mother agency gets a model a job that is *not* good for a model to do but just wants the money, it could ruin a model's career. Strategic marketing such as this is mostly needed for the high-fashion sector of the modeling world. A mother agent gets a percentage of your fee (even when you are in a foreign country) from the agency that you are with at the time, so they are also helping to "manage" your career worldwide. There are active mother agents, and not so active ones who solely collect a percentage because they discovered a model. This is a touchy phrase; please understand it fully before you agree that someone will be your "mother agent."

MODEL MANAGEMENT

Most of the larger agencies are "model *management* companies." If you work with one of these agencies then you would not *need* an active manager because they have the skills to get you work and manage your career. If you do have a manager, though, and they place you with an agency like this, your manager still plays the same role in handling your career, and the agency will simply just get you work and leave the "managing" up to your manager. In this case, the 20 percent commission a model agency takes from your wages will be split with the manager you employed.

AGENCY VERSUS MANAGER

The difference between a model "agent" and a model "manager" is that managers are not licensed to book work directly for you, unless you are working with a "model management" *agency*. Usually an agency is enough to get you started in the modeling world, but managers can help you market yourself more accurately because, if they are good, they speak to every agent in just about every market. Be careful, because sometimes managers take out more of a percentage than they are supposed to, and after the 20 percent commission the agencies charge, you do not need extra commission taken away from you on top of that. Some managers and agents split the 20 percent commission, as is the case if your manager is your mother agent as well—it depends on how the manager works with a particular agency.

Marketing yourself to a personal manager to help you get representation with an agency is fine; managers can help mold a career for you when you are not sure what to do next. But please investigate that manager thoroughly. Get references from modeling agencies and other models, use search engines like Google or Yahoo! to look up his or her name, and find out all you can, because you do *not* need a license to be a manager. Anyone can call himself or herself a "manager."

Also, not to confuse you, but be really careful with the word "manager." Sometimes modeling agencies call their bookers or agents "model managers." You need to make sure that you get the specific title of anyone who you are speaking to in the industry—if they are in any way vague with you, then they are probably trying to hide something.

The words "manager," "scout," and "agent" are all thrown around in different ways and can mean different things all of the time, depending on who is saying them. I have covered their definitions thoroughly, so the best way to find out exactly what someone does in the modeling industry is to look at their business card, and then make certain to check out their references thoroughly. Do not ever be afraid to ask too many questions. There are too many scam artists out there trying to fool you with their misleading statements. Ask the manager or whoever you are in contact with outright: "Do you book work for models?" or "Will you be paying me directly after you take commission, or will I be getting paid directly and giving *you* commission?" Agencies and managers work in different ways to pay their models for work that they get. Do the same thing if someone approaches you in a public place to become a model—be direct, ask specific questions, and research them thoroughly.

EXCLUSIVE VERSUS NONEXCLUSIVE

Some of the contracts and/or agreements are exclusive, and some are nonexclusive. Smaller markets will often have nonexclusive agreements for you to sign, so when an agency gets paid, they take their commission, but you are still allowed to get work from other agencies in that same area. Commercial print agencies have nonexclusive agreements as well. High-fashion modeling agencies will more than likely have exclusive contracts, meaning you cannot work with any other agency for high-fashion jobs in the geographical area where the agency is located. When I was a high-fashion model in Miami and doing commercial print work at one point, I had three commercial print agencies and was not allowed more than one high-fashion agency. It all depends on what market you are in, what kind of print work you are expected to get, and what kind of agency is going to select you.

ADVANCE

This is an amount of money your agency gives you (usually interest free, it depends on your agreement with the agency) on the premise that you will eventually pay it back with the work you acquire. You should ask about advances before you join an agency, as well as if the agency charges interest on advances. Will they advance the payment for a job? This is important, because it often takes two to three months for a client to pay. Will they advance the tests and composites? The agency Web site maintenance fee? If you are not in your hometown, will they advance money for food and transportation? (These types of advances are more common in larger cities.) Will the agency advance accommodations? (This is *very* common if you do not live in the city in which you are working.) How about advancing a plane ticket? Or laser copies of pictures in your portfolio, and also for the copies of portfolios that are left at the agency for clients to see? More and more of the marketing is digital, but it is a good thing to know if you are going to be charged for the extra copies of your portfolio that the agency uses to market you when you are not around. All these questions will help you be your own manager. An agency advancing you money is great, but you can rack up a huge debt if you are not careful, and you will be responsible for eventually paying it back, even if you do not make a profit in that market.

OPTION

An option is when a client wants to hold time on you, in other words, they would like to save a day or more on your chart for a potential job. You will get plenty of options, but only book some of them. Clients like to put options on more girls than they need, so they don't end up with no one for their shoot. So if you sign up with an agency and start getting "options" right away, then you know that agency is working for you, and it will most likely be a good market for your type of look.

BOOKING

Hopefully you will get plenty of these! A booking is just another word for "job," and it can range from not getting paid anything at all, to megamoney bookings for six figures and more. An agent will tell you that you are "booked" on a certain day or days, and it means that you are going to be working. First, along comes the option, and then after that hopefully the booking confirmation. When you go on vacation, or are sick, or have some other personal reason why you can't work or go on castings that day, then you will have to "book out" that day or days.

VOUCHERS

If you join and/or sign a contract with an agency, they will give you a "voucher book" at that time. This is for both you *and* the agency. A voucher is an informal agreement between you and the clients that you work for. It is similar to an "IOU." The voucher states what job you did, the date, and how much money you made for the day. (Advertising usages and royalties are a separate issue.) When you are finished with the job, you will ask the client to sign the voucher for you. After it is signed by you and the client, you will take it to the agency to be turned in to the agency's accounting division. After accounting logs it into their records, they will bill the client for the money, plus a 20 percent fee *on top* of your day rate that the agency gets to keep (as a service charge), *besides* the 20 percent they take out of your pay. So, if you work for $2,000 (which is an average starting catalog rate), your agency will make $800 off of you, that is, unless the agency has to give a percentage to a mother agency or a manager. Keep a copy of every voucher, so you can keep track of what the agency owes you financially.

AGENCY COPY

(AS ATTORNEY IN FACT FOR)

MODEL NAME:

DATE OF JOB: / /   PO. NO.

PRODUCT   STUDIO

RATE   TIME:

BILL TO: FROM: TO: $

ADDRESS: TRAVEL TIME: $

CITY   USAGE $

STATE   ZIP CODE

ATTENTION: AGENCY FEE TO BE ADDED TO THE TOTAL AMOUNT.   AGENCY FEE $

CHARTER MEMBER OF IMMA

SPECIAL BILLING/P.O. #:   TOTAL $

UNIFORM MODEL RELEASE (VALID UPON PAYMENT)

In consideration of receipt of the model fee (inclusive of service fee) as well as any additional usage fees negotiated with my manager, I hereby sell, assign and grant to _____ and _____

Advertising Agency or Publication   Client/Advertiser

the right and permission to copyright and use or publish one (1) photograph or likeness of me in which I may be included in whole or part of composite or reproductions thereof in color or otherwise in the United States for _____ usage: i.e. Print, POS, Pkg, OOH, etc. for _____ months to begin no later than four (4) months later than this date, except that these photos may not be used on TV in any manner. Accordingly, I release and discharge the company and persons named above and persons acting for or on behalf of them from any liability by virtue of any blurring, distortion, alteration, optical illusion, or use in composite form that may occur or be produced in the taking of said pictures or in any processing thereof through completion of the finished product. Note: Products, packaging usage, billboards, point-of-sale, hang tags, exclusivity, endorsements, use of name, TV and any other special usage require separate negotiations. All other releases not valid unless countersigned by model manager. Client's workman's compensation carrier is _____ .

CLIENT'S SIGNATURE _____   MODEL'S SIGNATURE _____

SAMPLE BLANK VOUCHER

BOOKER

This is slang for the term "model agent." The most up-to-date and politically correct way to label someone who is going to sign you to an agency and get you work is "model manager," and even though a "model manager" works in a modeling agency, he or she is not your "personal manager." Don't get too caught up with the "management" vocabulary in this sense. If you have any question as to what a person does, request that he or she differentiate themselves from the definition of a "manager" or "agent." If someone is working at a legitimate modeling agency, they are an "agent," and they are going to get you work. Personal managers are a totally separate entity. The most important thing that you have to be aware of is that the person who is asking to represent you has a valid place in the industry, and they are reputable. "Booker" will always be used as a term for someone who works in an agency and accrues work for the models, and if you use it with people in modeling agencies, they will figure out that you know more than a little about the business than the rest.

COMPOSITE

Composites are lightweight cards measuring approximately five inches by eight inches—every agency varies—with a few of your best pictures on them, along with your name, height, measurements, and your agency's contact information. I showed you some examples of models' composites in chapter 1. Often referred to as "comps," they have a function similar to that of a business card in other industries. When you go on a casting call, you will leave one with the client so they remember who you are. Composites go one step further than a business card though and are used to market you to clients by the agency. When a client calls an agency for a "comp pull," an agent will put together a tailored package for the client, depending on what type of models they request, and will either send it by messenger over to the client's office, send it in the mail, or by e-mail. Recently there has been a lot of digital marketing, where agents can e-mail your composites and/or portfolios as well, but a good many casting directors still want to see hard cards. A modeling agency will also do a mailing on you when you get a composite, to let clients know you are available for work.

GO-SEES

I taught you the difference between castings and open calls, but when you join an agency you will have "go-sees" as well. A go-see is just what the term says; it is an appointment for you to "go and see" a client. The only difference is that there is no particular job that the client is casting for at the moment. Models are often too casual about go-sees, because they are not for a specific job. But a client may have consistent work where they are casting all year, and they keep composites on file for when they need them, or another type of client may consist of a magazine or photographer who wants to keep track of the up-and-coming faces. Agencies work hard on getting you in front of clients, and go-sees are one way of doing that. A lot of clients do not want to bother with go-sees, but it is a good way to stay on top of which models are in town, and how the modeling industry is advancing.

MODELS' APARTMENT

You will find that agencies in the larger cities have what are called "model apartments" or at least a deal on a weekly or monthly basis with a local hotel. If you find an agency in a place where you are required to move, ask if they have a models' apartment, where it is, and what it costs. Be prepared for tight quarters, as they can be extremely busy at certain times during the year, such as during fashion show season, or the summer, when school is out and the younger models flock to the big cities to try their chance at the brass ring. A typical models' apartment in New York City is a two-bedroom, one or two bath apartment with four to eight girls staying there at one time.

PORTFOLIO OR "BOOK"

Your portfolio is the protective carrying case for your modeling photos. Agencies have portfolios that are more like hard-backed photo albums, as opposed to an artist's portfolio, the ones that are leather bound and have handles. The portfolio covers that have the agency's name on them can cost up to fifty dollars for each one, so when they hand you one, ask the price. A portfolio is typically charged to your account without the agency asking your permission. It is usually a requirement for you to walk around to castings or go-sees with one of the agency's portfolio covers, but to keep track of your expenses, there is no reason you cannot ask them how much it costs. Also, a common term for your modeling portfolio is a "book"; so if someone in the industry asks you for your "book," do not hand over the novel you have been reading at the beach!

A Word to Parents

It would be best for parents of children under the age of eighteen to read this entire book, as it is applicable to you, since you will be legally and financially managing your child's career until he or she reaches the age of eighteen. If your daughter or son signs a contract with an agency and she or he is only seventeen, the contract is useless, and it may affect you financially in the long run. You might have trouble getting paid for jobs that your child did, or at least it may cause payments to be delayed. Modeling agencies work like anyone else—if they can hold your money, they will! Agencies need your permission and signature for anything having to do with minors. So it is advantageous to learn as much as you can about the business, and this book gives you a good head start.

The process for marketing a child is the same as it is for adults. When I tell people not to spend money on professional pictures, it is even *more* important for parents of younger children. They grow and change so much that by the time you get the pictures taken and then processed, they may have changed again! Plus, even after you join a kids' agency (unlike one for teenagers and older), any agency specializing in children will *still* tell you that you do not need professional pictures! They can (and will) sell your son or daughter to their clients without professional pictures.

And just as with older models, children *must* live in the vicinity of where their castings are going to be. It is even more important for children, because the parent is going to be the one carting the child back and forth on go-sees, castings, and callbacks. There is a lot of running around to do, and the parent will be responsible for getting a child there on time and prepared for whatever the casting or audition requires (type of clothing, memorizing lines, etc.). Don't bother to send a child's picture in to an agency that is far away, unless you are planning to move there immediately. A modeling career for a child entails the same hard work as for adult models, and it is impossible to do that from long-distance.

DO YOUR RESEARCH

If an agency tries to un-involve you, let that be a warning sign. If they are a legitimate company, they should be more than happy to make you comfortable and accommodate any and all questions concerning your child. Do get referrals from other people, and ask to see the agency's Web site or an agency book when looking for representation for your child. The various search engines on the Web, such as Google and Yahoo!, will help you find out things about whom you are dealing with. Type in the agency's name, then in a separate search the *owner* of the agency, and any other background the agency may give you. You can also go to www.bbb.org to see if a company has had complaints against it, but if you cannot find the company or manager you are searching for complaints about in the Better Business Bureau, it does not necessarily mean they are not reputable.

Always go in person to see the agency's (or manager's) office itself. In the case of managers, get referrals and meet with the manager at length. Managers are good for children under eighteen, because the acting and modeling businesses go hand in hand, and a manager can get more business for you in commercials, film, and television, whereas a modeling agency focuses only on print work. A manager (not an agency, mind you) does *not* need a license to be in this business, so referrals from agencies are a good start. If you are in contact with a manager first, ask him or her what modeling or acting agencies he or she works with or is affiliated with, and call the agencies to inquire about that individual.

If you want to research an agency in the United States, first you need to find out if the state government (where the agency is located) *requires* a license for modeling agencies or not, then look up if the agency has a license, if required, or ask to see the license at the agency itself—licenses are supposed to be prominently displayed. You can check out both of these things at your local Department of Consumer Affairs. I tried it myself for the city of New York on their Web site and found the "talent" agencies under the subject of "employment agencies." Some modeling agencies were listed there as well, although it is a little confusing when you first start to navigate your way through the site. Keep looking, and if you don't find what you need, try another source like your state Consumer Protection Agency or the attorney general's office for previous complaints or warnings against a particular agency. It's good to take the time to do your research *and* ask the potential agency that you are in contact with about their history, such as how many years they have been in business, etc.

In addition, modeling agencies can provide referrals, whether it is from a client of theirs or from one of their model's parents, which are sometimes the best source. Again, no one will be annoyed at your checking up on them, and if they are, they probably have something to hide.

If your son or daughter is considering Europe, help them research whatever agency is interested in representing them, and follow up on whatever references you can get from that agency. If he or she is trying to get work in the high-fashion industry, Europe will have to be a consideration eventually. There are plenty of great agencies out there that take good care of models when they are abroad, and it can be an amazing opportunity for your son or daughter, not one that everyone is fortunate enough to experience.

If your son or daughter is over eighteen years old and wants to be a model, the best advice I can give you is to try to be involved in your child's career. Just because a girl or boy is over eighteen doesn't mean that they can figure out the intricacies of such a career as modeling, especially if he or she has moved to a larger city to experience life as a model. They will be trying to learn the modeling business, and at the same time figuring out life in a big city, and it can be a lot for a person to manage, especially without a support group such as their family or a close friend living in that city. Keep in touch with their agency and try to find out as much as you can about his or her living quarters. Also, review any legal documents that your son or daughter is asked to sign.

IMPORTANT RULE

Never leave a child under eighteen years of age in a room—with the door shut and/or no window—with just one other person! In other words, do not let your child go into a room for an appointment or audition with just one other person if you cannot see what they are doing. This advice is *not just for females*. No matter what your child's gender, be overly protective of any child working in the modeling or entertainment industry—it is the only way. I am certainly not trying to scare you, but if you watch the news and read the papers, pedophiles come in every shape, size, and color. Also, never leave a girl under the age of eighteen at a photo shoot without supervision. Your teenager may not like this but, believe me, it is a good idea to keep close tabs on what everyone on the set of a photo shoot is doing.

MIND GAMES

One sensitive issue that I would like to bring up to parents is your child's perception of herself as she begins to be exposed to the modeling industry. These thoughts are more for the teenage female models, as eating disorders and mental insecurity are rampant at this age and go hand in hand. I just want to comment on my personal experience, which hopefully will shed some light on what a tricky mental game modeling can be.

I was always a very skinny person naturally, and as a teenager I never had more than the average insecurities about my looks or weight. When I started in the modeling business in New York City as a brand-new model at the age of twenty, I was put in a models' apartment to live with *eight* other girls from the same agency in a two-bedroom apartment, *eleven* girls during show season. *All* of these girls had to work at keeping their weight down, and the topics of conversation in the apartment were mainly about weight issues or partying at the nightclubs, and at twenty years old, I was *by far* the oldest person in the apartment.

After a while, because I was surrounded by those in a career that was based on looks and size—when you are modeling in the high-fashion world, weight and age are *huge* issues, don't let anyone tell you any differently—I was told to lie (by my agency) about my age at twenty years old so people would think I was sixteen or seventeen at the most. I started thinking nonstop about my body and my weight, and when I was a few years older, I started obsessing about my age. Twenty-two is *ancient* for the high-fashion industry, because 99 percent of the high-fashion models are under the age of twenty-three, and when you are told over and over again that you are too "sophisticated"—which is a nice word for "old" in the modeling industry—you start to live it as well. Fortunately, I never had a problem that escalated into an eating disorder or a mental issue regarding my weight or age, but I saw how unbelievably *easy* it was to fall into that. No wonder celebrities feel so much pressure to stay skinny! I felt the pressure every day, and I was not in the public eye a fraction as much as a celebrity.

The reason I am telling you about this is because your child needs to be mentally prepared and very secure with herself to hear people who say constantly (to the *same person*), "You're too skinny," or "You're too fat" or "Your chest is too big" or "Your chest is too small" or "You're too tall" or "You're too short" or "Your hair is too short" and in another minute "Your hair is too long." Of course, people don't *mean* to get personal or be vicious, but clients in the modeling business get so caught up in what they are trying to sell, that they will consider your daughter a product right along with whatever they are marketing, and not even realize that they are hurting a person's feelings in the meantime. I have experienced this over and over again, and as an agent, I have seen the effect on insecure girls. The only thing you can do is to try and prepare for the outcome with your daughter. She should be told to take nothing personally, and whatever comments she may hear along the way are just comments, and there is nothing she can do about it. Warn her that people may be unintentionally harsh or critical, and she should try and have a thick skin. Also, a good way to prepare her is to establish a fitness and nutrition plan *before* entering into the modeling world, so she is in control of her weight and in good shape from the beginning. Working out in some form is always good for anyone, mentally and physically.

YOUNGER CHILDREN

Do you have younger children not ready for the adult modeling world? Keep this book! If your child is too young for high-fashion print work, yet you think he or she may have potential, this book will show you what to do when your child reaches that level, if he or she is not with a high-fashion agency already. Sometimes even if he or she already *is* with a high-fashion agency as a kid, they will *not* accept them automatically in their high-fashion division when they are old enough. I have met plenty of teenage models looking for representation who were already with high-fashion agencies, but as a teenager were not accepted into the high-fashion new-faces division at that same agency.

What age should you start looking at high-fashion agencies? Well, that depends on the height of your youngster. For girls, the age range where high-fashion agencies start becoming interested is around twelve to fourteen years old. If your daughter is a minimum of five seven by the age of twelve or thirteen, then that is a good sign. By the time a girl reaches fifteen though, she should be a minimum of five eight. And the measurements that I listed in chapter 1 are not negotiable, even if the child is younger—actually, *especially* if the child is younger. The way a high-fashion modeling agency thinks about younger kids and their weight is this: the older a girl gets, the more weight she will gain, and they usually stop growing in height at around seventeen years of age. Now, this is not necessarily what the medical world would tell you, because there are exceptions in every case, but it is a general rule that the agents use for weeding out potential models. If a girl is barely making the measurement standards for a high-fashion model at the tender age of fifteen—meaning, if she isn't thin enough—then a modeling agency will take into consideration that there may eventually be a weight issue. You have to remember that for every one girl that is taken into a high-fashion agency, there are *thousands* who are not accepted. If a girl is five seven and seventeen years old, a high-fashion agency probably won't even look at her pictures, as opposed to a girl who is five seven and thirteen years old, and who is within the physical measurement requirements of a high-fashion model.

As far as boys are concerned, high-fashion modeling for them really doesn't start until they are seventeen or older. Again, the height factor is the first deciding issue in whether or not a younger male has a chance at modeling. If a potential male model is not *at least* five eleven by the time he is seventeen, then there is a lot less of a chance that he will get representation for high fashion. Height is much more of a concern for males than it is for females in the modeling industry. Where the height of five

seven may be an exception here and there to the five-eight height minimum for females, being below the height of five eleven and a half inches
for male models is hardly ever an option. And the height window is very
narrow! If a male is over six two, then it suddenly becomes much more
difficult for them to find representation. And of course, they also have to
be within the measurements that I listed in chapter 1.

CONSIDER TELEVISION COMMERCIAL ACTING

And finally, one more thing parents ought to know is that commercial
acting is great for kids, especially ones at a younger age, even if you
were only thinking about modeling. It gets the child out there and
meeting new people, and for the most part, children are not competing
with other children who have had private coaching, until you get into
the teenage years. When you are an adult actor, much more is expected
in the way of education and experience, so the acting world can be
much more fun and less stressful for a child. Also, a lot of talent agencies have print divisions as well. So when your kids are older, they already have invaluable experience on their résumé, which they may or
may not move forward with, but at least they have the choice to utilize
it or not for their future.

Basically the same marketing technique is used for children breaking into acting as into modeling. Just send in natural, *nonprofessional*
pictures, as I described in chapter 2, concentrating on the personality
of the child instead of getting the exact proper poses. It doesn't matter
how a child stands. What matters is the *energy* of a child for the acting
world. And there is no reason why you can't send in pictures to the
television and film division as well as the commercial division. Older
actors need résumés and have a harder time breaking in if they don't
have on-camera experience, but you have the advantage with a young
child, even if he or she does not have any experience, because résumés
are not expected. After getting representation, the financial obligation
for acting will be the same as an adult actor, as far as getting eight-by-ten
head shots printed, etc. You can get away without getting professional
pictures as a child in the *modeling* business, but serious child *actors* need
eight-by-ten head shots once they are approximately grade school age.

Good Luck!!!

We are now coming to the end of our strategic marketing process on how to be involved as a model in the modeling industry, and hopefully by now you are on your way to finding representation, or have learned enough to market yourself to the world in a way that is most beneficial to you. Hang in there! Although modeling can be a very glamorous career, most of it is hard work and takes determination.

Don't forget that the most important thing for you to remember is that you can't *pay* for someone to suddenly make you a model. Occasionally people do have success when they pay money for pictures before they get an agency, or pay for a modeling convention, but these people could have also entered the industry for free and did not need to waste their money. You can call any legitimate agency around the world and ask them if you need to send them professional pictures to be considered for representation, and they will tell you no. There *must* be some truth to that, right? Then once you are with an agency, you can spend all the money you like on pictures, and they will be put to good use to try and get you work.

Besides not giving money to people to make you a "star," the other point I would like to end with is to stay strong and not take anything personally. It's not going to be easy when people tell you that you are too "this" or too "that," but unfortunately that is an undeniable part of the whole business. You are constantly being compared to other people, and you naturally turn into a commodity that is being evaluated. When you are a model you are turning whatever you are modeling into a product, and making it a part of you in whatever you are advertising. Ms. Samersova said it correctly when she stated that the designers are looking for a "hanger." For example, in high fashion, models show off the couture designs of high-end designers; in the more mainstream print world models show off clothing and jewelry, and commercial print models show off products, so all of the above models end up becoming a type of "hanger"—or product holder—for what they are trying to show or sell.

Don't give up! Now that you have more information on what the modeling industry is all about, you will be fully prepared for what is coming at you, and how to react to it. The best way to get into *any* industry is to find out everything about it that you can. I have given you this knowledge by combining the expertise of modeling agents, owners of modeling agencies, model managers, and professional models with what you would learn in modeling schools and at conventions, along with my extensive background as a model, model agent, producer, and casting director, to show you the modeling industry from every angle, inside and out. So feel confident, do your best, and don't pay money to anyone up front before you get representation, *ever*.

CONTACT INFORMATION

■　■　■　■

Note: I have not included addresses here because agencies are continually moving, and you should be checking out the Web sites first anyway, to confirm the current address and select a division, before sending any pictures.

MODELING AGENCIES

Bella Agency
New York, New York
www.bellaagency.com
phone: (212) 965-9200
Submit pictures through their Web site.

Bleu Model Management
Los Angeles, California
www.bleumodels.com
E-mail pictures to submission@bleumodels.com
phone: (310) 854-0088

The Campbell Agency

Dallas, Texas

www.thecampbellagency.com

phone: (214) 522-8991

Submit pictures through their Web site.

The Diamond Agency

Orlando, Florida

www.thediamondagency.com

talent@thediamondagency.com

phone: (407) 830-4040

Directions USA

Greensboro, North Carolina

www.directionsusa.com

faces@directionsusa.com

phone: (336) 292-2800

The owner of this agency checks this e-mail herself!

Greer Lange Talent Agency

Philadelphia, Pennsylvania

www.greerlange.com

phone: (610) 747-0300

Submit pictures through their Web site.

Model Team

Hamburg, Germany

www.modelteam-hamburg.de

E-mail pictures to info@modelteam-hamburg.de

phone: (49) (40) 4141037

The owner of this agency promised me that this e-mail is checked frequently.

Nova Models

Baltimore, Maryland

www.novamodelsinc.com

E-mail pictures to novamodelscd@aol.com
phone: (410) 752–6682

Silver Model Management
New York, New York
www.silvermodels.com
E-mail pictures to newfaces@silvermodels.com
phone: (212) 966–1717

FIT MODELING AGENCY

Fit, LLC
No Web site—this agency prefers pictures by mail.
Send pictures and *exact* height and measurements to:
124 East 40th Street, #1103
New York, NY 10016
Fit, LLC, is a small agency that specializes in fit modeling, so there
is no need for an "attention to" on the envelope.

PROMOTIONAL MODELING

GC Marketing
phone: (212) 780–5200
To register for promotional modeling, go to www.gcmarketingser
vices.com.

EUROPEAN IMAGE MANAGEMENT

Talents Europe Management
www.talentseurope.com
Only for established artists. Do not send photos if you are a new
model.

AGENCY SUGGESTIONS FOR ITALY AND GERMANY

Beatrice International Models
Milan, Italy
www.beatricemodels.it
Women: e-mail pictures to womencasting@beatricemodels.it
Men: e-mail pictures to mencasting@beatricemodels.it
phone: (39) (02) 4692599

Fashion Models
Milan, Italy
www.fashionworld.it
E-mail pictures to info@fashionmodel.it
phone: (39) (02) 480861

Women Management
Milan, Italy
www.womenmanagement.it
Main division: e-mail pictures to info@womenmanagement.it
New-faces division: e-mail pictures to info@namesmodel.com
phone: (39) (02) 47719557

Model Team
Hamburg, Germany
www.modelteam-hamburg.de
E-mail pictures to info@modelteam-hamburg.de
phone: (49) (40) 4141037

Okay Models
Hamburg, Germany
www.okaymodels.com
E-mail pictures to email@okaymodels.com
phone: (49) (40) 3785000

Harry's Models
Munich, Germany
www.harrys-models.com
phone: (49) (89) 3600000
Submit pictures through their Web site.

PHOTOGRAPHERS

Alexey Yurenev
www.alexey-studio.com

Signe Vilstrup
Repped by www.tomorrowmanagement.com

Fadil Berisha
www.fadilberisha.com

David Kaptein
www.davidkaptein.com

Stanley Debas Photography
www.debasphotography.com

Ron Reagan
www.ronreagan.com

Scott Teitler
www.scottteitler.com

Lou Freeman
www.loufreeman.com

Floyd M. Dean
www.deandigital.com

MODELS

Chantal Bolivar

Contact Wilhelmina Models in New York City or go to www
.chantalbolivar.com.

Helen Powers

Contact Fit, LLC, in New York City or go to www.helenpowers
.com.

Shea Kravcak

Contact bellabird@mac.com for inquiries about modeling *only*.